VELOCIRAPTOR

PTERODACTYL

SPINOSAURUS

APATOSAURUS

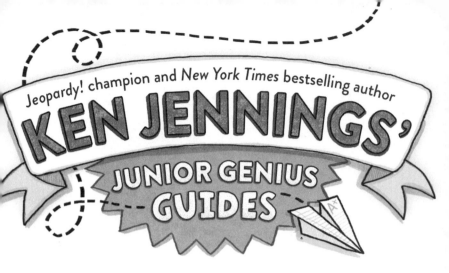

Jeopardy! champion and New York Times bestselling author

KEN JENNINGS'
JUNIOR GENIUS GUIDES

DINOSAURS

BY **KEN JENNINGS**

ILLUSTRATED BY **MIKE LOWERY**

SEMPER QUAERENS

LITTLE SIMON

New York London Toronto Sydney New Delhi

THE OFFICIAL
JUNIOR GENIUS CIPHER

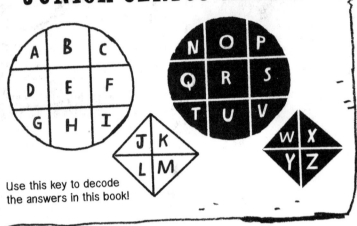

Use this key to decode the answers in this book!

LITTLE SIMON

An imprint of Simon & Schuster Children's Publishing Division
1230 Avenue of the Americas, New York, New York 10020
First Little Simon edition February 2016
Text copyright © 2016 by Ken Jennings. Illustrations copyright © 2016 by Simon & Schuster, Inc.
All rights reserved, including the right of reproduction in whole or in part in any form.
LITTLE SIMON is a registered trademark of Simon & Schuster, Inc.,
and associated colophon is a trademark of Simon & Schuster, Inc. For information about special discounts
for bulk purchases, please contact Simon & Schuster Special Sales at 1-866-506-1949 or
business@simonandschuster.com. The Simon & Schuster Speakers Bureau can bring authors to
your live event. For more information or to book an event, contact the Simon & Schuster Speakers
Bureau at 1-866-248-3049 or visit our website at www.simonspeakers.com.
Manufactured in China 1115 SCP
2 4 6 8 10 9 7 5 3 1
Library of Congress Cataloging-in-Publication Data
Jennings, Ken, 1974– author.
Dinosaurs / by Ken Jennings ; illustrated by Mike Lowery.
pages cm. — (Ken Jennings' junior genius guides)
Audience: Ages 8–10. Audience: Grades 4 to 6.
ISBN 978-1-4814-2956-6 (hc) — ISBN 978-1-4814-2955-9 (pbk) — ISBN 978-1-4814-2957-3
(eBook) 1. Dinosaurs—Juvenile literature. I. Lowery, Mike, 1980– illustrator. II. Title. III. Series:
Jennings, Ken, 1974– Ken Jennings' junior genius guides.
QE861.5.J48 2016
567.9—dc23
2015015523

CONTENTS

INTRODUCTION

Hello, my friends! I am your knowledge guru and all-around role model, Ken Jennings. You may call me Professor Jennings.

I can tell by your large brains and hairy heads that you are all mammals. Good job, everyone! It's great to be a mammal, isn't it? We have pretty much ruled the earth for the last sixty million years. But in today's class we're heading back into earth's prehistoric past, to find out who was running the show before the mammals. (Spoiler warning: You will not believe this, but IT WAS GIANT REPTILES!)

We have billions of years of prehistory and hundreds of different amazing dinosaurs to cover today. But even that huge amount of knowledge should be no problem for a Junior Genius. Remember, our official motto is *"Semper quaerens,"* which is Latin for "Always curious."

Before we leave the twenty-first century behind, let's say the Junior Genius Pledge! Place your right finger to your temple, face this drawing of Albert Einstein, and repeat after me!

With all my fellow Junior Geniuses, I solemnly pledge to quest after questions, to angle for answers, to seek out, and to soak up. I will hunger and thirst for knowledge my whole life through, and I dedicate my discoveries to all humankind, with trivia not for just us but for all.

All right, Junior Geniuses. I hope you like volcanoes, because when you turn the page, we're going to be on a very different earth.

FIRST PERIOD

THE LAND BEFORE TIME

History means "writing things down," Junior Geniuses. If nobody records something happening, historians will never know about it. Keep that in mind when a grown-up promises to get you ice cream "later" or "some other time." Get the promise in writing, or it didn't happen!

Human beings have been keeping written records for only five or six thousand years. Everything that happened before that is *prehistoric*—before history.

We all know how time in recorded history works: We use a calendar. Days, months, years, centuries. Prehistory is different. The dinosaurs didn't know or care if it was Tuesday or Friday or March or October.

Prehistoric time uses a geologic time scale, which scientists calculate based on evidence they find in rocks. Comparing geologic time to a modern calendar is like comparing a dinosaur to a flea: It's much, *much* bigger.

Geologic time is measured in:

AGES
(long spans of time, hundreds of thousands of years)
that combine to make up

EPOCHS
(really long spans of time, millions of years)
that combine to make up

PERIODS
(*incredibly* long spans of time, tens of millions of years)
that combine to make up

ERAS
(*amazingly* long spans of time, hundreds of millions of years)
that combine to make up

EONS
(*insanely* long spans of time, billions of years)

EARTH DAY

The problem with geologic time is that it's hard to wrap your brain around it. Think how long one minute can feel on the last day of school, or when there's not a vacant stall in the restroom and you're *desperate*. Now try to imagine one billion years' worth of minutes. Good luck!

But I have a trick that may help. Let's compress the entire life of the earth down to one twenty-four-hour day. Blink your eyes once. BOOM, more than five thousand years just passed. All of human history, and you missed it. That's how fast time is going on this scale.

If the earth has been around for only one day, it was pretty busy.

12:00 A.M.: Earth forms out of dust and gas swirling around the sun.

4:00 A.M.: Life! Microscopic one-cell organisms appear in the oceans.

1:00 P.M.: Not until after lunch do these cells start to have a nucleus and little organs.

6:30 P.M.: Around dinner, tiny multi-cell creatures.

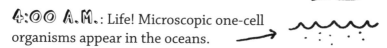

8:30 P.M.: The first plants— simple seaweed.

8:50 P.M.: Right around bedtime, animals finally explode onto the scene. Jellyfish!

9:50 P.M.: Animals and plants evolve onto land.

10:20 P.M.: Insects! Reptiles!

11:00 P.M.: Dinosaurs rule the earth.

11:40 P.M.: The dinosaurs disappear, and mammals take over.

11:59 P.M.: Human beings evolve and eventually develop farming, the Great Pyramids, democracy, and, finally, the *Junior Genius Guides*.

That's the time scale we're talking about. Pretty much all of human evolution is the last minute of the day. Sixty seconds. Two TV commercials.

So it's not all about us.

A DIFFERENT WORLD

For the first billion years, earth was a lifeless rock. But that doesn't mean it was boring. Here are some things you should not do if you ever travel back in time to visit the earth of more than 4 billion years ago.

Remember not to . . .

Breathe! The atmosphere has no oxygen. Unless you're a fan of poisonous gases such as carbon monoxide, ammonia, and methane, hold your breath.

Walk anywhere! Do you like that playground game where you pretend the ground is lava? Well, here the ground is *literally* lava. Even once the earth's rocky crust forms, giant volcanoes are everywhere.

Get wet! Once rain starts to fall and the oceans appear, they are heavy on sulfuric acid instead of oxygen.

Go outside! A hail of asteroids and comets is hammering away at the earth, pulled by some mysterious chaos in the orbit of the other planets.

On second thought, maybe it's not a nice place to visit at all.

COMET RELIEF

Of course, we might not be here today if not for those icy comets. When they smashed into the earth, they delivered water that helped make life possible.

SOUP-ER MODEL

We don't know exactly how life first appeared on earth, but it was a long, slow process. In the 1950s, a group of scientists combined four simple chemicals (water, methane, ammonia, and hydrogen) and heated and cooled them while zapping them with electricity. Within weeks the mixture had started to form *amino acids*, the molecules that make up the proteins in living cells.

Could the same thing have happened across millions of years as lightning struck the prehistoric ocean? (Sometimes scientists call this liquid the *primordial soup*, which does *not* make me hungry for soup.) And could those complex molecules have eventually evolved into early proto-cells? It seems possible. Other scientists think that the first life to arrive on earth may have hitched a ride aboard comets or meteorites. If that's true, we are all space aliens.

In any case, life appeared before the earth had its billionth birthday. We've found fossils in Australia that show evidence of one-third-inch-thick mats of microbes more than 3.5 billion years old.

SUDDENLY SHELLFISH

Over time these tiny cells got better at being alive, through a simple kind of evolution. They developed different parts that would do different things, such as produce energy, process chemicals, or store food. After another billion years, creatures very much like the bacteria and algae we know today were bobbing in the prehistoric ocean.

THE TIME BEFORE LAND

During some of that time, we think that earth turned into a water world, with the oceans covering 98 percent of the surface! There were also eras when earth was a giant snowball. During those times, even the equator was covered in ice and muddy volcanic ash.

But evolution took a *long* break at that point. For the next billion years the only form of life on earth was some slimy gunk. And I mean "slimy gunk" in the most respectful way possible, because these are our ancestors I'm talking about here! Scientists call this time period the *boring billion*.

But the boring billion ended with a very un-boring bang, about 530 million years ago. This event is called the Cambrian explosion, and it looked exactly like this:

TRILOBITE
JELLYFISH
OPABINIA

Okay, it wasn't an actual explosion. But during just ten million years—and remember, that's a very short amount of geologic time—most of the major kinds of ocean life we know today appeared practically at once. These are critters that would look right at home next to modern starfish, sponges, and shrimps. Many had shells. Some had eyes. The first *vertebrates*—creatures with backbones, like us—evolved then too, in the form of simple, wiggly fishlike creatures.

What was the billion-year holdup? For the answer, let's go to a new Junior Genius feature I like to call Ask a Trilobite.

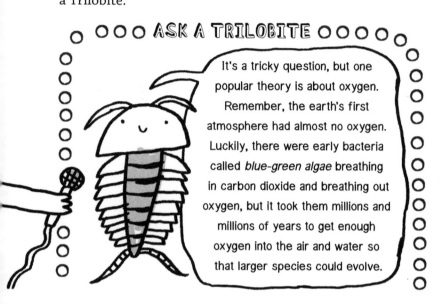

OOO ASK A TRILOBITE OOOO

It's a tricky question, but one popular theory is about oxygen. Remember, the earth's first atmosphere had almost no oxygen. Luckily, there were early bacteria called *blue-green algae* breathing in carbon dioxide and breathing out oxygen, but it took them millions and millions of years to get enough oxygen into the air and water so that larger species could evolve.

FISH OUT OF WATER

The Cambrian explosion began the Paleozoic era, one of the three eras of life we can study through fossils. Each one ended with a massive extinction. (Except ours, luckily! Fingers crossed.)

PALEOZOIC
(FISH)

MESOZOIC
(DINOSAURS)

CENOZOIC
(YOU!)

During the Paleozoic, which ended about 250 million years ago, animal life finally made it out of the oceans. The first to try dry land were the *arthropods*—animals with hard outer skeletons and jointed legs, like today's crabs, spiders, and insects. Their bony exoskeletons acted like reverse scuba suits, so they could explore land without drying out.

BUG-EYED MONSTERS

Some of the scariest creatures ever to live on earth were Paleozoic arthropods. *Jaekelopterus* was a massive sea scorpion with eighteen-inch-long claws that it used to snatch prey. On land, *Arthropleura* was a millipede more than eight feet long—the size of a crocodile!

Soon some fish began to develop fins that would help them scramble up rivers in search of food, and it turned out those scrambling fins could do something new and cool called walking.

LIKE...

WHOA!

GIVE ME EIGHT!

As these fish became *amphibious* (able to live in water *and* on dry land), they adapted to their new surroundings. Some had a set of gills, for breathing underwater, *and* a set of lungs, for breathing air. And eventually the soft, squishy eggs of amphibians evolved into the harder eggs of reptiles, so the animals could lay the eggs on land without the eggs drying out.

We know from fossil footprints that some of the early amphibians had seven or eight toes on each fin-foot, but the most successful of them must have had five, because almost all *terrestrial* life today has five fingers and five toes. You are probably holding this book with five-fingered hands right now, unless you're a cartoon character, like Mickey Mouse.

LOOK IT UP!

POP QUIZ!

Animals were probably already exploring dry land before plants started to grow there. The first land plants were relatives of what small modern plant, which you might see growing in mats on trees and rocks?

REPTILE HOUSE

"Yes!" you are probably saying right now. "It's only page 17 and he's already gotten to the good stuff:

DINOSAURS!

That was totally worth the first fourteen boring pages about single-celled algae and trilobites and stuff!"

Well, I'm afraid we're not quite to the dinosaurs yet, Junior Geniuses. I'm going as fast as I can, but we've got billions of years to deal with here.

Did you know that not all prehistoric reptiles were dinosaurs? Did you further know that, at the same time that early reptiles were evolving into dinosaurs, they were also evolving into mammals like us? Let me explain.

Reptiles evolved in the swampy Carboniferous period, a geological period that ended 300 million years ago. That's 100 million years *before* dinosaurs appeared on the scene. The first reptiles we know of were less than a foot long and looked a lot like modern lizards.

One reptilian family, called synapsids, was the ancestors of modern mammals. Being a lifelong mammal yourself, you probably know that most mammals:

HAVE FUR OR HAIR • GIVE BIRTH TO LIVE YOUNG ARE WARM-BLOODED • PRODUCE MILK FOR THEIR YOUNG

But none of those are things that show up in fossils. Luckily, synapsid fossils do contain other clues telling us how reptiles turned into mammals—such as the changing shape of their jaws, and the addition of tiny inner ear bones to help them hear better.

To our modern eyes, lots of these reptiles were lizards *shaped* like mammals.

LYCAENOPS (WOLF LIZARD)

PROCYNOSUCHUS (OTTER LIZARD)

PLACERUS (HIPPO LIZARD)

EXTRA CREDIT

A synapsid called *Oligokyphus* looked so much like a weasel that scientists assumed for decades that it was a mammal. Nope! It was a reptile.

TRIASSIC WORLD

About 250 million years ago, a massive extinction ended the Paleozoic era and began a new era, the Mesozoic, the age of reptiles.

We don't know what caused the catastrophe, and maybe we never will. But a lot of the synapsids died. Many of the reptiles that thrived after the big extinction were the bigger, stronger ones—like the archosaurs.

The archosaurs are the ancestors of modern crocodiles and birds. And in the late Triassic period, some archosaurs evolved into a new kind of lizard—the dinosaur.

Hold your horses, kids. Let's learn more about what the earth was like when the first dinosaurs lived.

Let's imagine that you're packing a backpack for a trip to the Triassic period. Even with your best supplies, you might be in for a surprise. You'd have to be careful using . . .

A WATCH. It would always be wrong, as a day was less than twenty-three hours long in the Mesozoic era. The earth's rotation has slowed down a bit since then.

A COMPASS. During much of the age of reptiles, compasses would have pointed south! The earth's magnetic field has reversed hundreds of times since then, back and forth from north to south.

MATCHES. Watch out when lighting a fire! From studying air bubbles trapped in amber (a kind of hardened tree resin), scientists guess that the earth's atmosphere back then was 30 percent oxygen, much more oxygen-rich than it is today.

MAPS. **Don't bring a GPS! You wouldn't even recognize the planet earth of 250 million years ago.**

Here's why:

THE RIGHT PLATES AT THE RIGHT TIME

The earth's continents sit on massive shelves called *tectonic plates* that float on a layer of gooey molten rock. But these plates can move around over time, crashing into or sliding under one another.

In the Permian period, 250 million years ago, all the plates were stuck together in one big continent, which we call Pangaea ("pan-JEE-uh"), meaning "all land."

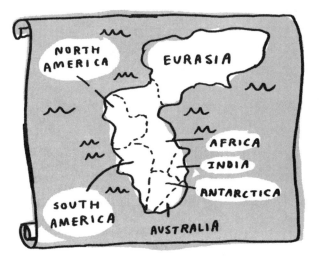

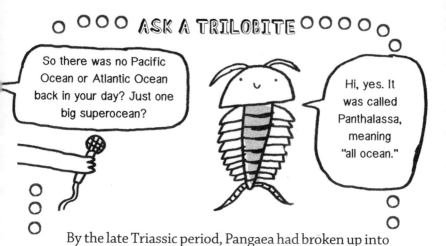

So there was no Pacific Ocean or Atlantic Ocean back in your day? Just one big superocean?

Hi, yes. It was called Panthalassa, meaning "all ocean."

By the late Triassic period, Pangaea had broken up into two great landmasses called Laurasia and Gondwanaland.

LAURASIA

GONDWANALAND

By the Cretaceous period, our modern continents were taking shape. Most of central North America was underwater, part of the shallow Western Interior Seaway.

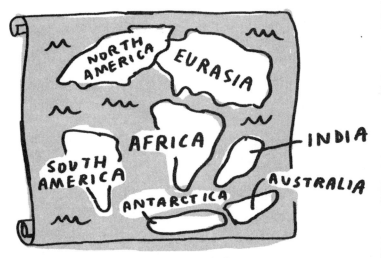

Eventually we got to the world that we see in our atlases today.

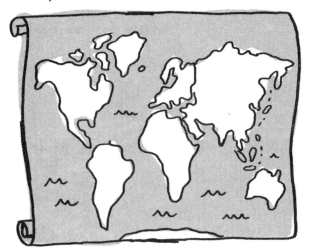

This map might look the most familiar to you, but it's definitely not the end of the story!

Geologists predict that in 250 million years, the continents might once again collide to form a new super-continent, called Pangaea Ultima.

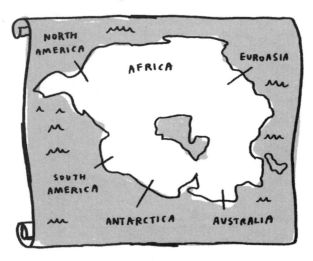

If any traces of New York City still stand in 250 million years, they won't overlook the Atlantic Ocean. They'll be right next to southwest Africa!

EXTRA CREDIT

Because of these changing continents, fossil hunters today find matching species in places as far apart as Portugal and Wyoming. In the Triassic period, the Atlantic Ocean hadn't opened up yet.

NOT LAWN FOR THIS WORLD

This dance of the continents meant that reptiles in the age of reptiles lived in a topsy-turvy world. Antarctica was toasty warm. The Sahara, today a barren desert, was once a lush forest.

O OOO ASK A TRILOBITE OOOOOₒ

Wow! So what were the oceans like during dinosaur times?

How should I know? I went extinct way before that.

But a lot of the earth *was* a hot, dry desert during the Triassic period. Life mostly flourished along the coasts, where the weather was milder. During the Jurassic period, things got cooler and wetter, but the climate was still warmer than the earth we know today. In fact, there were no polar ice caps at all during the Cretaceous period.

Plant life was very different too. On a Triassic nature walk, you'd see some plants you recognized:

FERNS

CYCADS
(SIMILAR TO PALMS)

EVERGREENS

But the surprise is what you wouldn't see. No grass! No leafy trees or bushes! In fact, no flowering plants at all! They all evolved millions of years later.

A lot of modern animals had already evolved. By the end of the Cretaceous period, the earth's forests were full of frogs, snails, ants, worms, and even opossums. There were dragonflies during the Mesozoic era too, but with one big  difference—their wings were longer than a human arm!

This is the world that the dinosaurs ruled.

DINOSAURS! FINALLY!

SECOND PERIOD

DAY OF THE DINOSAURS

Many people probably imagine a scene like the one above when they hear the word "dinosaur." But Junior Geniuses should know better, because that battle pictured is impossible! *Tyrannosaurus rex* and *Stegosaurus* never met. *Stegosaurus* died out in the Jurassic period, 80 million years before the first *T. rex* evolved.

Dinosaurs ruled the earth for an *incredibly* long span of time, Junior Geniuses—more than 160 million years. We actually live closer to *T. rex*'s time than *T. rex* did to *Stegosaurus*'s time!

Take another look at that timeline, because it'll make you smarter than a lot of grown-ups. Believe it or not, 41 percent of American adults in a recent poll thought that humans and dinosaurs lived together at the same time! Actually, the only place humans and dinosaurs ever lived together was on *The Flintstones*.

EXTRA CREDIT

Dino, the Flintstones' pet dinosaur, was originally voiced by actor Mel Blanc, better known as the voice of Bugs Bunny, Daffy Duck, and dozens of other Looney Tunes cartoon characters.

STAND UP STRAIGHT!

What makes a dinosaur? They're giant, scaly, slow-moving reptiles, right? Well, scientists once thought so, but today we know better.

GIANT? The big, mountain-size dinosaurs may get all the attention, but actually the average dinosaur was about the size of a car. Some were as small as a chicken.

SCALY? Dinosaurs did have scaly skin, but it was more like bumpy bird skin than that of a modern snake or crocodile. On most—possibly even all—dinosaurs, the scales evolved into feathers.

SLOW-MOVING? Ever see a modern iguana sunning itself on a rock? Most dinosaurs probably had much faster metabolisms than that lazy lizard, making them more like today's warm-blooded mammals and birds. Lots of dinosaurs, like predators, were probably scary quick.

REPTILES? Dinosaurs are a kind of reptile, but not like any you'd see around today. Let's find out why.

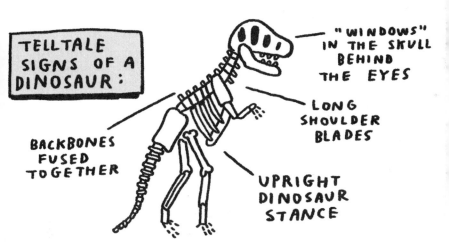

TELLTALE SIGNS OF A DINOSAUR:

"WINDOWS" IN THE SKULL BEHIND THE EYES

LONG SHOULDER BLADES

UPRIGHT DINOSAUR STANCE

BACKBONES FUSED TOGETHER

The way a dinosaur stands is really the giveaway. Modern reptiles have legs that sprawl outward. (Okay, except for snakes, smart aleck.) But dinosaurs evolved upright legs, just like mammals have today. This posture helped them run faster and for longer periods.

Let's travel down a dinosaur from head to tail like a paleontologist would, studying the fossils for clues to what dinosaur life would have been like.

FOSSIL FOOLS

Herrerasaurus, with its long, narrow skull, probably had a simple, primitive, tube-shaped brain. So it wasn't exactly the sharpest fossil in the rock formation. But let's face it, none of the dinosaurs were exactly rocket scientists.

About 85 percent of your brain is made up of the cerebrum, where you do all your higher thinking. But dinosaurs had tiny cerebrums. Almost all of a dinosaur's brain was used for simple survival tasks, like senses and movement.

By comparing the skull cavities of dinosaur fossils, scientists can guess which dinosaurs were dumber than others. Instead of IQ, they use a measure called EQ, which stands for "Encephalization Quotient." The EQ compares an animal's *actual* brain size to the brain size you'd expect, given its body mass. It's a way to guess at intelligence. Humans, of course, have the highest EQ.

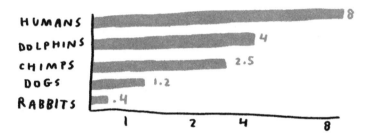

Dinosaur EQ turns out to be *very* low, with some of the biggest dinos clocking in at just 0.1. *Stegosaurus* was the size of a school bus, but had a brain about the size of a golf ball. Don't ask *Stegosaurus* for help with a crossword puzzle, is what I'm saying.

For more than a century, paleontologists believed that *Stegosaurus* and other dinosaurs might have had a second brain most of the way down their spinal column, which would have helped run their back legs and tails. A brain in their butt, in other words. But we know now that whatever this mystery butt organ did, it wasn't for thinking. (It probably stored energy in the form of sugar.)

LIZARD MEN RUN THE WORLD!

As dinosaurs evolved, they did get smarter, with brains more like modern birds' than like reptiles'. A small Cretaceous dinosaur called *Troodon*, a clever hunter, was one of the smartest. One scientist has suggested that if the mass dinosaur extinction had never put mammals in charge, earth might by now have been ruled by Dinosauroids, humanlike descendants of the *Troodons*!

LOOKING GOOD

It wasn't just *Stegosaurus*. *All* dinosaurs were sort of dumb. But what was going on inside a dinosaur's skull was often a lot less interesting than what was going on *outside*.

That's because many species of dinosaurs had surprising horns, crests, and frills on their heads. These probably were brightly colored and were used for display—to help dinosaurs identify others of the same type, and possibly the opposite sex. Think of these horns and crests as the Mesozoic version of a peacock's tail, or a very showy hairstyle.

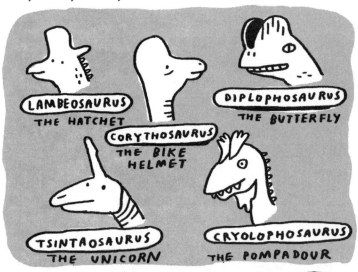

LAMBEOSAURUS
THE HATCHET

DIPLOPHOSAURUS
THE BUTTERFLY

CORYTHOSAURUS
THE BIKE HELMET

TSINTAOSAURUS
THE UNICORN

CRYOLOPHOSAURUS
THE POMPADOUR

EXTRA CREDIT

Cryolophosaurus was originally called *Elvisaurus* by its discoverer, because its crest looked like Elvis Presley's famous hairdo.

THANK YOU. THANK YOU VERY MUCH.

Some of these unusual heads might have had other uses *besides* looking cute to the opposite sex. Big showy crests and frills might have helped dinosaurs regulate their temperatures. The animals may have turned the crests toward the sun when they needed to warm up, or dumped heat in the shade on a hot afternoon.

Pachycephalosaurus was a dinosaur that always used its head . . . especially in a fight. It had a ten-inch domed skull that it could smash into rivals' heads or sides like a battering ram while the dinosaur was fighting over mates or territory.

But some dino skulls still remain a mystery. *Muttaburrasaurus*, which was discovered in Muttaburra, Australia, in 1963, had a big, weird bump on its snout. Did this hollow chamber help it make loud noises? Increase its sense of smell? No one is sure.

EXTRA CREDIT

Pretty much all the nitrogen and hydrogen and oxygen in our biosphere has been here for hundreds of millions of years. So take a deep breath. You now have the very same molecules in your lungs that the dinosaurs breathed! Now pour a glass of water. Every drop has been through a dinosaur's kidneys probably many times! Enjoy that refreshing glass of dinosaur pee.

BIG EATERS

Traveling down the skull, we get to the eating parts of the dinosaur: its teeth or bill, its neck (a thirty-foot neck, in some cases!), and its digestive organs.

Most dinosaurs ate plants—scientists guess there were thirty times more *herbivore* (plant-eating) dinosaurs than *carnivore* (meat-eating) ones. And eating plants took up a *lot* of the dinosaurs' time. The biggest long-necked dinosaurs would have needed to find more than half a ton of food . . . every day!

HOMEWORK

Next time you're hungry, choose a leafy snack, like a salad. Considering that the average salad weighs four ounces, how many salads do you think you'd have to eat to satisfy a *Diplodocus* for the day? Remember, you'll need half a ton of veggies to do the trick. Grab a calculator and see if your guess was close.

Dinosaur jaws adapted to the food they ate.

Brachiosaurus had teeth like thin spoons, for snipping tough leaves.

Diplodocus had long, thin pencil-shaped teeth, for stripping vegetation off branches, like with a comb.

Psittacosaurus had a parrot-like beak, for chomping into fruit and nuts.

JUNIOR GENIUS
VOCABULARY BOOSTER

Beaked dinosaurs probably had bills made out of a protein called *keratin*. That's the exact same stuff your fingernails are made of!

The duck-billed dinosaurs had the weirdest mouths of all—and more teeth than a whole *herd* of *T. rexes*. *Nigersaurus* went through its hundreds of teeth like candy, replacing each one every two weeks or so. *Edmontosaurus* had sixty rows of closely packed teeth— more than a thousand teeth in all! Maybe the dinosaurs

went extinct because their dental exams took so long.

But some dinosaurs had such terrible table manners that they didn't chew at all! Long-necked dinosaurs saved time by gulping their food down whole. Many dinosaurs had a grinding organ called a *gizzard*, just like modern birds, crocodiles, alligators, and seals do. They would swallow rocks, some as big as softballs, and the rocks would squish around with food inside their muscular gizzard, "chewing" it up.

CRACK A WINDOW!

Millions of vegetarian dinosaurs produced so much burping and farting that it might actually have caused global warming! One team of scientists estimates that dinosaurs produced 570 million tons of methane every year, as much as humans and our livestock do today. Dinosaurs may have made their world into a more tropical—not to mention smellier—place.

EGG-CELLENT

All dinosaurs reproduced by laying eggs, but *egg*-zamples of fossils from different species can be *egg*-stremely different. The smallest known dino eggs were found in Thailand. They were smaller than sparrow eggs, measuring less than an inch across.

ACTUAL SIZE

The largest eggs, on the other hand, were football-shaped and were nineteen inches long! That's two or three times bigger than any ostrich egg. Now, that may sound pretty huge if you're making an omelet, but it's still smaller than you might *egg*-spect for a dinosaur. After all, a fifty-ton animal was going to be *egg*-spanding from that little egg. Some long-necked dinosaurs grew to more than twenty-five thousand times their size as hatchlings. So why were dinosaur eggs so *egg*-ceptionally small? Because if they got any bigger, their shells would have been too thick for a baby dinosaur to *egg*-splode out of.

EGG-STRA CREDIT

In 2012, fossil hunters in Chechnya reported an *egg*-citing new discovery: dinosaur eggs approximately three feet long! But when these "eggs" were *egg*-zamined by Russian scientists, they turned out to be . . . round rocks.

Fossil *egg*-sperts have *egg*-sposed groups of as many as twenty-one dinosaur eggs at the same site. Dinosaurs must have had *egg*-straordinarily large families! Some of these clutches of eggs were found with adult dinosaur fossils in actual nests, so at least some dinosaurs *brooded*—sat on their eggs to keep them warm and safe from predators that might want to *egg*-sterminate them. In one *Maiasaura* nest, we've even found fossilized chewed-up plant material, which may have been used by the mama lizard to feed her newly hatched young. That's how *Maiasaura* got its name, which means "caring mother lizard."

Okay, that's enough with the egg jokes, I'm eggs-hausted

ROAD TRIP!

Even once the babies were hatched, we think that many dinosaur families stuck together. Some beds of fossil bones contain thousands of dinosaurs of the same species, so we assume they traveled in herds. In fact, there are "trackways" of fossilized footprints—dinosaur highways—that show us that dinosaurs protected smaller herd members by keeping them on the inside, the same way elephants travel today.

Some of these dino road trips were long migrations, maybe sixteen hundred miles each way.

THE TAIL END

We end our *l-o-o-o-ong* journey down the dinosaur body at the tip of the tail. In the biggest known dinosaurs, we've traveled 120 feet from the head at this point, longer than a baseball diamond.

Since fossilized dinosaur footprints don't come with dragging-tail marks, we know that dinosaurs, unlike Godzilla, walked with their tails upright—even the ones with very long tails. *Diplodocus*, one of the biggest long-necked dinosaurs, had a forty-five-foot tail with seventy-three different bones in it. A forty-five-foot tail seems like it might be annoying to carry around all the time, but just think of all the things *you* could do if you had one.

GET COOKIES FROM THE TOP SHELF.

Even some of the biggest dinosaurs liked to rear up on their hind
feet to reach the juiciest vegetation high up in the prehistoric
trees. Their long tails helped them
balance while they snacked.

AVOID BUG BITES.

You've seen a cow swish its tail to keep flies off? Dinosaurs probably did the very same thing. And it's a good thing they did. We've found Jurassic bugs trapped in amber, and they are no fun. When dinosaurs got fleas, they were mega-size ones with beaks as thick as doctor's syringes!

SCARE OFF BULLIES.

Apatosaurus's tail tapered down to the width of a human thumb at its tip. Scientists calculate that it was so thin that *Apatosaurus* could have cracked it like a whip with very little effort, frightening predators with a *BOOM!* louder than a massive naval cannon.

POP QUIZ!

Whips—and maybe dinosaur tails—make a loud crack because their tip is going faster than what?

THE SPEED OF SOUND

MYSTERIES OF PREHISTORY

We know an amazing amount about the dinosaurs, Junior Geniuses, considering that no human being has ever seen one—or ever will. But lots of very basic things about their lives are still unknown. Paleontologists are still putting together the puzzle pieces of evidence.

Here are my top five favorite unsolved dinosaur puzzles—and our best guesses as to the answers.

Warm-blooded or cold-blooded? There's growing evidence today that dinosaurs had active metabolisms and their bodies could generate heat. For example, we think that many dinosaurs grew fast, stood up straight, hunted at night, and lived in cool climates. These are all traits of warm-blooded creatures, but it's also possible that many dinosaurs were cold-blooded and relied on warmer climates and their larger size to keep their body temperatures stable.

How long did they live? The life spans of modern birds and reptiles vary quite a bit, so we think dinosaur lifetimes did too. The larger ones could have lived

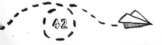

for a century or two, if they were anything like modern tortoises! We just don't know.

What color were they? Because we mostly have fossils of dinosaur bones, not soft tissues, there's still a lot that we don't know about how dinosaurs looked. Did they have cheeks? Lips? We're not sure. The colors of dinosaurs you see in books and movies are only guesses, but that's changing. Microscopic study of fossilized skin and feather cells can actually tell us which pigments those cells produced! In 2010, *Sinosauropteryx* became the first dinosaur whose color we know something about. It had an orange back and white stripes on its tail.

Did males and females look different? Typically scientists have no idea whether fossils are from male or female dinosaurs. Sue, the famous *T. rex* skeleton in Chicago's Field Museum, might actually be male, who knows? Call him Stu, I guess. In 2005, for the first time, paleontologists were able to pin down a fossil's sex by finding *medullary bone*, a tissue that female dinosaurs' bodies used as a calcium source to make eggshells.

How did their circulatory systems work? It's very rare, but sometimes dinosaurs' fossils show traces of blood vessels. We've never found a heart, though, so we have to imagine what it might have been like. One study calculated that pumping blood up a long *Diplodocus* neck would require a heart weighing 1.6 tons! That's heavier than a lot of cars, so it's probably not true. Did dinosaurs have some other kind of pump or siphon system helping out their hearts? We're still trying to figure it out.

Who knows, Junior Geniuses? Maybe someday you'll be the paleontologist who solves one of these mysteries.

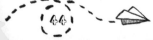

We're taking a break from dinosaurs so you can spend a few minutes here in the Holocene, which is the name of our current geologic epoch. But if you were having too much fun in the prehistoric past to come home, here are a few ideas for dinosaur games you can play with friends. I'll see you all back in class when the bell rings!

EVOLUTION

This is a great way to watch life on earth evolve in a matter of minutes. All players start out as single-celled bacteria, wiggling randomly around the room making realistic bacteria noises. As you move around, every time you run into another player, you play a single game of rock-paper-scissors. The winner advances one step up the evolutionary ladder, while the loser "devolves" one step. The ladder looks like this:

HUMAN. You win!

GORILLA. Hoot and holler and pound on your chest.

RODENT. Look around worriedly with paws up, and smack your rat teeth.

DINOSAUR. Roar and flail your little *T. rex* arms.

FISH. Pucker up your lips and swim with your fins.

BACTERIA. I'll be honest with you—this is the most boring stage.

Players who successfully evolve into humans are out of the game and can go do human things like get a snack or watch TV. Once exactly one player remains in each of the other stages, the game is over.

DINOSAUR NEST

This game is just like hide-and-seek, only in reverse. One player hides while everyone else closes his or her eyes and counts. After one minute the other players scatter out to look for the player who hid. But when each seeker finds the hider, he or she doesn't announce it! Instead, the seeker hops into the hiding spot, joining the hider. Soon everyone will be huddled together like dinosaur eggs in a nest. The game ends when the last person finds the dinosaur nest. Then everyone can "hatch" and the last seeker becomes the new hider.

If you're playing at night, try the game indoors with all the lights turned off!

PAULINE THE PALEONTOLOGIST

Let's face it, Junior Geniuses, a lot of dinosaurs have long, hard-to-remember names. That's why you know a lot more dinosaurs than your parents or teachers probably do. Grown-up brains are too full of things like bills and online passwords to remember the really important stuff, like how to pronounce *"Epidexipteryx."* [1]

Here's a game that will test your memory *and* teach you some new dinosaur names. Sit in a circle and take turns clockwise adding to the fossil finds of Pauline the Paleontologist.

The first player says "Pauline the Paleontologist got back from the fossil beds, where she dug up a *Triceratops*." (Or whatever dinosaur he or she chooses.)

The second player adds a dinosaur. "Pauline the Paleontologist got back from the fossil beds, where she dug up a *Triceratops* and a *Brachiosaurus*."

Each player must remember the full list and add one of his or her own. "Pauline the Paleontologist got back from the fossil beds, where she dug up a *Triceratops*, a *Brachiosaurus*, and a *Velociraptor*."

If you get lost or mess up the list, you're extinct! The last player left is the winner.

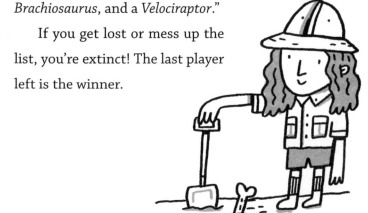

[1] EP-ih-dex-IP-teh-ricks

THIRD PERIOD

ALL CREATURES GREAT AND SMALL

For a true dinosaur lover, the best time to be alive would have been the Mesozoic era, of course. (Except that you probably would have been eaten very quickly.) The *second* best time to live would be . . . right now! Junior Geniuses, we are living in a golden age of dinosaur discovery.

Paleontologists today are discovering and naming a new dinosaur every two to three weeks! A 2006 study predicted that scientists will someday discover 1,844 different dinosaurs—and we know about only 500 of them so far. That means about 71 percent of all the types of dinosaurs who ever lived are still out there waiting to be found. At the current rate, we have 150 years of amazing new discoveries waiting for us!

We shouldn't be surprised that those discovered dinosaurs include an amazing array of different sizes and shapes. After all, here in the age of mammals, the mammals look very different. You look very little like an elephant or a coyote or a platypus, and *nothing* like an ele-yote-pus (a combination of the three that I just invented in my head).

Well, there was just as much variety back in the age of reptiles. Let's find out just how much.

HIPS DON'T LIE

There are two main divisions of dinosaurs—the *saurischians* ("lizard-hipped") and *ornithischians* ("bird-hipped"). This is a reference to the shape of the dinosaur's pelvis bone—is it pointed forward, like a modern lizard's, or backward, like a bird's? Ironically, we now know that modern birds are descended from the lizard-hipped dinos, not the bird-hipped ones!

Every other kind of dinosaur you can think of is a variety of either saurischian or ornithischian. You can always figure out which by answering just two questions!

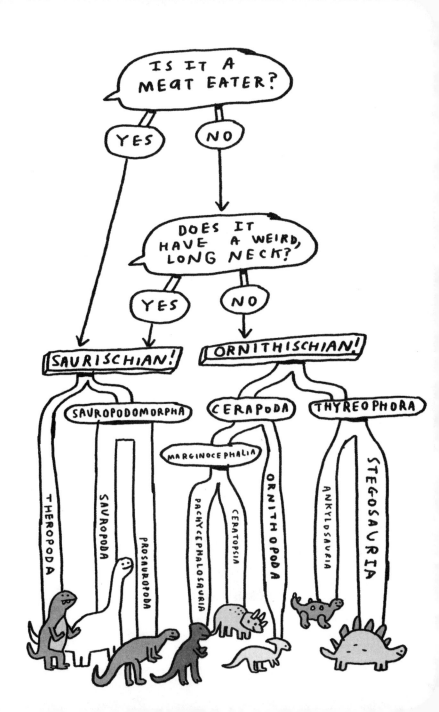

Some of those groups have pretty long names, but I can make it simpler for you with this Official Junior Genius Guide to Dinosaur Classification. Please clip out the box below, memorize it, and eat it.[2]

OFFICIAL JUNIOR GENIUS GUIDE TO DINOSAUR CLASSIFICATION

Theropods. Bipedal (standing on two legs), carnivorous dinosaurs, from *Velociraptor* to *Tyrannosaurus*.

Sauropods. Long-necked dinosaurs, such as *Brachiosaurus* and *Diplodocus*.

Stegosaurs. Dinosaurs with bony plates and spikes down their backs and tails.

Ankylosaurs. Bulky, armored dinosaurs.

Ornithopods. Bipedal grazers, like the duck-billed dinosaurs.

Ceratopsians. Beaked dinosaurs, most with facial horns and frills.

Pachycephalosaurs. Bipedal dinosaurs with thick, domed skulls.

[2] Just kidding. Do not cut up or eat this page, especially if it's a library book!

GIANT STEPS

The largest creatures ever to walk the earth—by far!—were the long-necked sauropods. *Brachiosaurus*, for example, was as tall as a four-story building when it lifted its head all the way up, and it weighed as much as twelve elephants. Its footprints could be five feet wide, long enough for you to lie down and take a nap. (As long as you were sure the dinosaur wasn't coming back again!)

Scientists are just as amazed by these barn-size dinosaurs as you are. How did they get so big, and why? We think that their over-size bodies helped them to survive by letting them reach more food sources and protecting them from smaller predators. If most animals got that big, they'd just collapse under their own weight, but dinosaurs had some specialized body parts that allowed them to supersize.

MOM, THE SAUROPOD IS STANDING ON ME AGAIN, AND HE WON'T STOP!

SPECIALIZED BODY PARTS AHEAD!

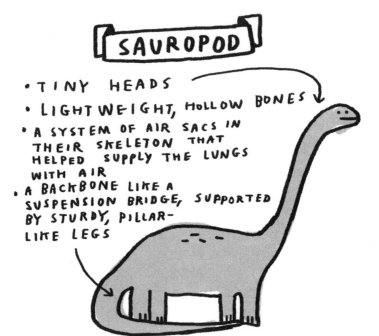

SAUROPOD

- TINY HEADS
- LIGHTWEIGHT, HOLLOW BONES
- A SYSTEM OF AIR SACS IN THEIR SKELETON THAT HELPED SUPPLY THE LUNGS WITH AIR
- A BACKBONE LIKE A SUSPENSION BRIDGE, SUPPORTED BY STURDY, PILLAR-LIKE LEGS

EXTRA CREDIT

As big as they were, some long-necked dinosaurs were bipedal—they walked around on their hind feet! *Plateosaurus*, an early ancestor of the sauropods, weighed more than four tons, but it could stand and used its strong, five-fingered hands to grab food.

Because we usually dig up dinosaurs just a few bones at a time, it's hard to be 100 percent sure what the one

biggest dinosaur was. In 1979, hikers in New Mexico discovered the bones of a sauropod that paleontologists named *Seismosaurus* and estimated it to be the biggest dinosaur of all time. The skeleton was so big, it took eight years to  dig it up! Unfortunately, as they worked, the scientists gradually discovered two things about *Seismosaurus*:

1. It wasn't as big as they thought.
2. It wasn't a new dinosaur at all. It was just an unusually large *Diplodocus*.

Oops.

So who *is* the undisputed heavyweight size champ of the dinosaur world? It might very well be a mysterious sauropod called *Amphicoelias*. *Amphicoelias*'s *femur* (thighbone) and a *vertebra* (backbone) were discovered in Colorado in 1877, and excited paleontologists realized that they might belong to a dinosaur twice as long as *Diplodocus*. That would make it more than 150 feet long and 110 tons in weight. But we might never know for sure! The bones mysteriously disappeared shortly after they were first studied, and have never been seen since.

Until *Amphicoelias*'s bones turn up in a lost-and-found somewhere, here are the other big players in the sauropod game:

Sauroposeidon could raise its head fifty-six feet above the ground. That's as tall as three giraffes stacked up. (If you could get three giraffes to do that.) It was named for Poseidon, the Greek earthquake god—and with good reason. The ground literally shook when *Sauroposeidon* went for a stroll.

Argentinosaurus is believed to have weighed more than one hundred tons, as much as a medium-size airliner. That would make it the second-heaviest animal ever to live on earth, after only the blue whale.

Mamenchisaurus was a funny-looking sauropod. Its telephone-pole-length neck measured fifty feet, half the length of its entire body! Its neck, which contained a whopping nineteen bones, was probably stiff, so *Mamenchisaurus* would have held

it horizontally. If you were meeting *Mamenchisaurus* for coffee, you'd see its weird, tiny head, about the size of a horse's, more than a minute before its hindquarters showed up.

A **Giraffatitan** in a natural history museum in Berlin, Germany, is the largest in the world. It's a seventy-three-foot-long giant dug up in Africa, and it's virtually complete.

LARGEST MOUNTED SKELETON

WELCOME BACK, BRONTOSAURUS!

Brontosaurus had one of the coolest names of any dinosaur: "thunder lizard" in Greek. Unfortunately, it didn't get to use its cool name for over a century.

Here's what happened: In 1903, scientists decided that *Brontosaurus* was actually the same dinosaur as *Apatosaurus* ("deceptive lizard"), a specimen that had been dug up a couple years earlier. So *Brontosaurus* got renamed *Apatosaurus*. In science, unfortunately, ties are broken by the earliest name, not the coolest one.

But in 2015, a new study found that *Brontosaurus* actually had a narrower neck than *Apatosaurus*, so it was a different species after all. It got its cool name back!

IT WAS A SMALL WORLD AFTER ALL

Not all dinosaurs were giants. The skies and swamps and forests of the Mesozoic era were also filled with flocks of tiny dinosaurs, some as small as a modern pigeon.

It's hard to be sure which was the *very* smallest. For many years the smallest dinosaur specimen known was the chicken-size *Compsognathus*, found in Germany during the 1850s. But we know now that the tiny German specimen was actually a *young Compsognathus*. The adults were a bit bigger.

EXTRA CREDIT

Compsognathus is one of the few dinosaurs whose exact diet we know. Two different skeletons have been found with tiny lizard bones fossilized in their bellies. Both must have died shortly after a delicious lizard dinner.

Two of the smallest dinosaurs known today are the feathered *Microraptor*, found in China, and the omnivorous *Fruitadens*, found in North America. Both weighed about two pounds, about the same as a jar of peanut

butter. Many dinosaurs had *teeth* taller than these little guys!

During the late Cretaceous period, the place to be if you were a small dinosaur was a large island called Hateg, which is now part of the eastern European country of Romania. For whatever reason, *Tyrannosaurus*-size predators never reached Hateg, so the dinosaurs that lived there began to shrink in size. (Without a need to defend themselves, smaller animals often thrive, because they need less food and territory.) The result? An island full of adorable dwarf dinosaurs! Species such as *Europasaurus* and *Magyarosaurus* were shaped just like giant sauropods, but shrunk down to about the size of a cow!

FORTY-POUND WEAKLING

Another surprisingly shrimpy dinosaur was *Coelophysis*. This early carnivore was ten feet long, almost as long as a small car, but it weighed less than you do! Built for speed and agility, *Coelophysis* had hollow bones and amazingly scrawny legs, neck, and tail.

CATCH ME IF YOU CAN

Coelophysis wasn't just the size of a car; it was also as fast as one. It's hard to be sure about dinosaur speeds, since we missed seeing them in action by millions of years. How do we even guess? We look at their footprints!

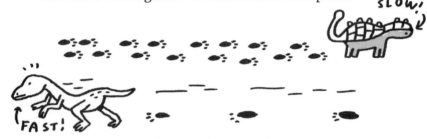

By measuring the space between dinosaur footprints, and comparing it to what we know about the length of the dinosaur's legs, we can guess how fast they were moving. *Coelophysis* might have gotten up to twenty-five or thirty miles per hour, but it wasn't the fastest dinosaur. Take *Struthiomimus*, a long-legged Cretaceous dinosaur that looked sort of like an ostrich with arms and a tail. *Struthiomimus* had nothing to worry about from any predator, since it could outrun them at speeds of up to fifty miles per hour!

With their long, muscular legs, bigger dinosaurs, such as *Tyrannosaurus*, were probably also able to run fast. But muscles aren't everything! Lots of big carnivores had little wimpy arms, which means they had no way to catch themselves if they tripped or fell. As a result, some scientists think *Allosaurus*, for example, never ran faster than a human jogger. It just would have been too dangerous.

HOMEWORK

Mark off a specific short distance (one hundred feet, maybe) and have someone time you running it. Calculate your average speed. Could you have outrun a *Stegosaurus*? Their top speed was probably around four or five miles per hour.

THE UGLY TRUTH

Let's be honest. We think dinosaurs are cool because they *look* cool. The spikes, the teeth, the giant claws and necks and tails. But isn't that just a little bit shallow? Let's look below the surface and give equal time to the *weirdest*-looking dinosaurs. I bet they have inner beauty.

Dinosaur:
Epidendrosaurus
Weird feature:
One *super*long finger
On the plus side:
Good for scratching fleas

Dinosaur:
Pelecanimimus
Weird feature:
Throat pouch, like a pelican
On the plus side:
Could save snacks for later

Dinosaur:
Leaellynasaura
Weird feature:
Big, bulging eyes
On the plus side:
Could probably see in the dark

Dinosaur:
Linhenykus
Weird feature:
Stubby, little one-fingered arms
On the plus side:
Could clip nails superquickly

Dinosaur:
Spinosaurus
Weird feature:
A giant sail on its back,
taller than a person
On the plus side:
Good for looking cool
or staying cool.

Dinosaur:
Heterodontosaurus
Weird feature:
Three kinds of teeth:
tusks, chopping teeth,
and chewing teeth

On the plus side:
Could probably eat plants
and small animals

Dinosaur:
Qianzhousaurus
Weird feature:
A *Tyrannosaurus*-like head . . .
but with a long, thin nose!
On the plus side:
Got the nickname "Pinocchio rex"
from scientists

SIX MONTHS UNTIL MORNING

Leaellynasaura lived in Australia back when Australia was *much* closer to the South Pole than it is today. The climate wasn't as cold as modern-day Antarctica, but it still would have been dark for months at a time in the winter. We know dinosaurs lived there, so they must have adapted to this long night. They might have developed night vision, or learned to burrow into the ground.

JUNIOR GENIUS JOVIALITY

Q: What did *Leaellynasaura* wear to keep warm during those dark polar winters?
A: A Jurassic parka.

WHAT'S IN A NAME?

Want to have a dinosaur named after you? Sure, we all do! One option is to make sure your parents are paleontologists. The discoverers of *Leaellynasaura* named the new dino for their young daughter, Leaellyn.

If your parents don't dig for fossils on weekends, don't worry! There are other options. You could find a dinosaur yourself. In 2008, five-year-old Daisy Morris

was walking on a British beach when she stumbled on a fossil, which turned out to be a completely unknown kind of prehistoric reptile. Today, the species is called *Vectidraco daisymorrisae.*

You could also get famous and then wait for the paleontologists to come knocking on your door. (Or, hopefully, your agent's door.) There are prehistoric reptiles named for . . .

PHILOSOPHERS!
(Chinese thinker Confucius)

ARTISTS!
(painter Georgia O'Keeffe)

ROCK MUSICIANS!
(guitarist Mark Knopfler)

PRESIDENTIAL CANDIDATES!
(science advocate Ross Perot)

CONQUERORS!
(Mongol emperor Genghis Khan)

AUTHORS!
(*Jurassic Park* novelist Michael Crichton)

COULD YOU SPELL THAT FOR ME?

Jurassic Park is to blame for one of the worst dinosaur names ever: *Tianchisaurus nedegoapeferima*. That second word was coined by Steven Spielberg, who combined the last names of eight different *Jurassic Park* stars.

Many amazing dinosaur discoveries are being made in China, which has led to hard-to-pronounce names such as *Xuanhuaceratops* and *Zheijangosaurus*. But China has also given us the *shortest* dinosaur name on record, a genus of duck-size dinosaurs called *Mei*, meaning "to sleep."

The longest dinosaur name on record? That would be genus *Micropachycephalosaurus*. This little guy was one of the smallest dinosaurs, but its twenty-three-letter name sure is a mouthful.

Believe it or not, there are also dinosaurs named for

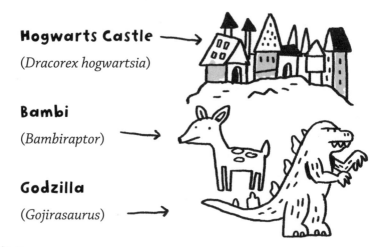

Hogwarts Castle ──→

(*Dracorex hogwartsia*)

Bambi

(*Bambiraptor*) ──→

Godzilla

(*Gojirasaurus*) ──→

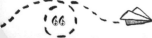

Naming dinosaurs can be tricky business, as it's not always clear which species are new and which are related. Poor *Allosaurus* has had *nine* different names over the years. But the real victims are the dinosaurs who get stuck with unfair names, such as these poor guys:

Brontomerus ("thunder thighs"). That's a pretty mean name for a dinosaur—especially one that was in such good shape! *Brontomerus* actually had more muscular legs than any other sauropod.

Mussaurus ("mouse lizard"). Named for its small size, but it turns out the early specimens were just babies. The adult "mouse lizard" was actually ten feet long. That's a big mouse.

Arrhinoceratops ("no-nose-horn face"). Actually, it does have a nose-horn. Oops.

Irritator (um, "irritator"). This dinosaur probably wasn't irritating in person. But the scientists who named it were annoyed that part of its skeleton had been faked by illegal fossil dealers.

Oviraptor ("egg thief"). The first *Oviraptor* fossils were found inches from a nest, so scientists assumed the dinosaur was stealing the eggs to eat them. *Very unfair!* The eggs turned out to be *Oviraptor* eggs. The poor dinosaur was just guarding her own nest!

POP QUIZ

If "*Oviraptor*" means "egg thief," what dinosaur do you think was named for the Latin words meaning "swift thief"?

My favorite dinosaur name is *Technosaurus*, which I think should look like this:

But, as we've seen, dinosaur names can be misleading. *Technosaurus* actually got its name in a pretty boring way. It was discovered at Texas Tech University. Oh, well. Maybe the robot dinosaur of my dreams is still out there . . . somewhere. . . .

ART CLASS

Every dinosaur who ever lived left only one skeleton behind, but it also left a lot of footprints during its daily strolls. Some of those tracks were baked hard by the sun and still survive today, either on the surface or buried under layers of rock. Dinosaur footprints are so common that they were discovered long before actual dinosaur bones. The first American scientists to notice dinosaur prints decided that the country must have been once filled with flocks of giant ostriches!

Today *trace fossils* such as footprints can tell us just as much as bones can about how dinosaurs lived. It's hard to match fossilized footprints to an exact species, so footprint samples get their own fossil names, just like dinosaurs do.

But even if we don't know what species they came from, footprints can be full of clues for smart dinosaur detectives.

- **How did this dinosaur stand?**

- **How much did it weigh?**

- **Was it walking or running?**

- **Did it travel in herds?**

- **Did it migrate?**

For example, in Glen Rose, Texas, in 1938 paleontologist Roland Bird found four large theropod tracks near a dozen sauropod tracks. The carnivorous theropods may have been stalking or even attacking the sauropod herd.

EXTRA CREDIT

In the 1990s, scientists in Sucre, Bolivia, discovered a three-hundred-foot limestone wall just *covered* in dinosaur tracks—far more than five thousand different prints. So were Mesozoic dinosaurs scaling the vertical cliffs of Bolivia, like Spider-Man? Sadly, no. This was once a flat, sandy shoreline that later got tilted upward by tectonic activity.

One of the best things about dinosaurs is that they got to stomp around with giant feet, making all the noise and destruction they wanted. You can do the same thing by making your own giant dinosaur feet! It's easy. All you need is:

DUCT TAPE

CRAFT PAINT

TWO TISSUE BOXES

KITCHEN SPONGE

CRAFT GLUE

First, if the tissue boxes still have tissues in them, you need to use up all the tissues. Catch a cold and sneeze a lot. If it's not cold season, watch a sad movie and cry your way through a lot of tissues. (Or you could find tissue boxes that are *already empty*.)

The openings in the tops of the tissue boxes need to be big enough for your feet to slide in but narrow enough that the boxes don't fall off your feet while you are crashing through prehistoric swamps. To make the opening smaller, use duct tape. You may want to cover the whole box with a layer of tape, for more durable dino feet.

Now it's time to decorate your new feet. Craft paint is one easy option. Or cover the box with decoupage glue and add "scales" of colored tissues. Remember, we don't know exactly what color the dinosaurs were, so you can be as creative as you want.

When the paint or glue is dry, it's time to add toenails. Cut an old kitchen sponge into triangles. (Cardboard or foam will work too.) Glue the triangles securely to the front of each foot. A grown-up with a hot glue gun might come in handy here.

How many toes? That's up to you. Sauropods had five toes on each rear foot, but *Triceratops* had four, and many carnivores had only three main claws.

Now it's time to get out there and start making trouble. *Dinosaur-size* trouble. But remember, if you start leaving rectangular tissue-box footprints all over the yard, you are really going to confuse paleontologists of the future.

FOURTH PERIOD

TOOTH AND CLAW

From what we've seen so far, the Mesozoic era was pretty chill. Herds of majestic animals, just eating leaves and laying eggs and whatnot. A peaceful paradise, right? Well, I'm sorry, but this is the chapter where we ruin all that. There's no getting around it. Sometimes dinosaur life got violent.

Dinosaurs ate one another. All the time. A lot of them were giant, cold-eyed killing machines. Monsters from your worst nightmares.

This chapter is rated PG. Reader discretion is advised.

PG PREHISTORIC GROSSNESS

- FOR INTENSE REPTILE ACTION
- SCENES OF BLOODY CARNAGE
- BRIEF CANNIBALISM

I AM THE LIZARD KING!

The most famous theropod (a bipedal, big-toothed dinosaur) was, of course, *Tyrannosaurus rex*. Even people who don't know what a theropod is know about *Tyrannosaurus rex*. Its name is Greek and Latin for "tyrant lizard king."

Let's take a close-up look at the lizard king. (Don't worry, we won't get too close.)

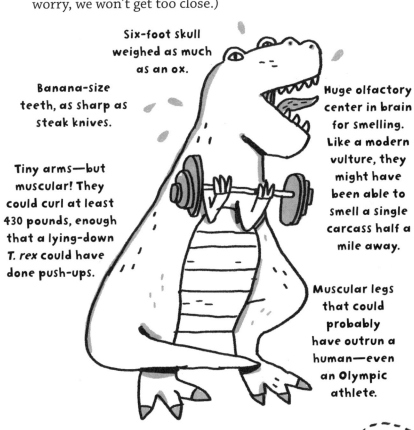

Six-foot skull weighed as much as an ox.

Banana-size teeth, as sharp as steak knives.

Tiny arms—but muscular! They could curl at least 430 pounds, enough that a lying-down *T. rex* could have done push-ups.

Huge olfactory center in brain for smelling. Like a modern vulture, they might have been able to smell a single carcass half a mile away.

Muscular legs that could probably have outrun a human—even an Olympic athlete.

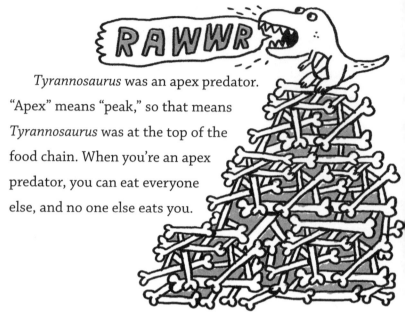

Tyrannosaurus was an apex predator. "Apex" means "peak," so that means *Tyrannosaurus* was at the top of the food chain. When you're an apex predator, you can eat everyone else, and no one else eats you.

Here are some modern examples of apex predators:

lion—

on the African savannah

polar bear—

on the icy tundra

Komodo dragon—

Wow, no idea. Komodo, I guess?

EXTRA CREDIT

Tyrannosaurus wasn't even the biggest apex predator of its era! We've discovered two other theropods from different parts of the prehistoric planet that were even bigger than *T. rex*—*Giganotosaurus* ("giant southern lizard," found in Argentina) and *Carcharodontosaurus* ("jagged tooth lizard," found in the Sahara).

LET US PREY

As top predators, *Tyrannosaurus* and other theropods were designed to do one thing: eat. Scientists think their massive jaws could bite down with a force of thirteen thousand pounds. That's three times as strong as any shark and fifty times as strong as a lion! Just one *CHOMP!* could be a force as powerful as an elephant sitting down!

Those mighty jaws and giant teeth meant that mealtimes were pretty quick in the *T. rex* household. Five hundred pounds of meat—about the equivalent of a modern steer—would go down the hatch in just one bite.

Tyrannosaurus ate its own weight in meat every week or so. It's possible that it fed the same way that lions do today—by filling up on a big prey animal when meat was available and then digesting for days.

Their little arms were strong but not long enough for fighting. So how did *Tyrannosaurus* attack its prey? Paleontologists studying *Triceratops* bones in Montana have found lots of unhealed *T. rex* tooth marks around the bony frill on *Triceratops* skulls. This means that *Tyrannosaurus* probably used its massive jaws to

SENSITIVE READERS: PLEASE SKIP THE REST OF THIS SENTENCE!

literally rip off the *Triceratops*'s head and eat the carcass from the neck down. Claws would come in handy for pulling off chunks of meat. Mmmmm!

EXTRA CREDIT

When it was dug up, the famous *Tyrannosaurus* skeleton Sue had the tooth of a different *T. rex* embedded in its neck. Perhaps hungry, hungry tyrannosaurs sometimes resorted to eating one another!

HUNGRY EYES

When the *Tyrannosaurus* attacks the jeep in *Jurassic Park*, the kids are warned to hold still, because "It can't see us if we don't move!"

Junior Geniuses, this is just terrible advice. If a *Tyrannosaurus* were coming at you, you would need to move. This probably wouldn't help since we think *T. rex* was a fast runner. But moving would definitely be better than holding still.

From what we can tell, *Tyrannosaurus*'s skull was designed for great vision. Their big eyeballs could probably see about thirteen times as sharply as yours, which means they could clearly see objects almost four miles away! They also had a wider field of vision than a hawk's.

As if you're not feeling bad enough about yourself, here are three more dinosaurs who could see better than you:

Troodon had big eyes, a big optic bulb in its brain, and good binocular vision. (That means it could see in 3-D.)

Gallimimus had eyes on opposite sides of its head, like a horse. That gave it almost 360 degrees of vision. It could even see behind itself!

Velociraptor had a large bony ring in its eyeball, which is usually a sign of a *nocturnal* animal—one that hunts at night. *Velociraptor* probably had amazing night vision.

ALL ABOUT THAT BASS

Tyrannosaurus had keen senses of sight and smell, but its weakness may have been its hearing. By studying the inner ears of birds, one paleontologist has decided that big dinosaurs could hear only very low sounds, such as booms and thumps and thuds. They might have been completely deaf to high-pitched sounds—such as the screams of their victims.

LEAPING LIZARDS

Tyrannosaurus had such a bone-crushingly strong jaw that it could even have dented car metal—if there had been any cars around to dent back in the Mesozoic era. (Bonus history fact: There were not.) *Allosaurus* was a smaller carnivore with a weaker bite, but just as scary.

An *Allosaurus* had about the same jaw strength as a modern leopard. But it had extra joints in its head that let it open its mouth *super*wide. Then it would bring its upper jaw swinging down, using its sharp teeth to chop into prey like an ax. So it could take quick bites while its dinner was still alive! Gross.

Today we are used to smaller animals being cuddly and nonthreatening. Dachshunds are cuter than Dobermans. Penguins are cuter than ostriches. Babies are cuter than linebackers.

But the prehistoric earth was *crawling* with predators that were smaller than *Tyrannosaurus* . . . and they were just as scary as the big boys.

Sinornithosaurus had grooved teeth, like modern snakes. Some paleontologists think it might have killed prey with a venomous bite!

Dromaeosaurus was tiny but had a retractable claw on each foot. It would leap into the air and slash at its prey, using its toe as a switchblade.

Deinonychus was the larger cousin of *Dromaeosaurus*. It had the same ninja toes, but was so big, it could make a three-foot gash with one swipe of its claws.

Another *Dromaeosaurus* cousin was *Velociraptor*. They were the clever, ferocious villains of the *Jurassic Park* movies. But Hollywood was lying to us *again*! Real *Velociraptor*s were only about eighteen inches tall, not human-size. (You can see why they scaled them up, though. Who would run from a poodle-size *Velociraptor*? Just say "Down, boy!")

But paleontologists have discovered a *real* scary raptor. The new specimen, which they named *Utahraptor*, was eight feet tall, as big as an ice-cream truck, and swiped at its prey with foot-long claws. Now *there's* your movie!

TIGERS OR WOLVES?

The scariest thing about Hollywood raptors is that they're smart enough to hunt in packs. In reality we're not sure if dinosaurs hunted alone (like tigers) or in groups (like wolves).

Deinonychus teeth have been found in the remains of much larger dinosaurs, such as *Tenontosaurus*. To bring home a big meal like that, *Deinonychus* must have been hunting in groups.

Not necessarily. Maybe the *Deinonychus* was targeting juvenile *Tenontosaurus*, or scavenging meat from an already-dead carcass.

But we've found lots of predator fossils together. One fossil bed in Utah had at least forty-six *Allosaurus*. They must have been hunting together, right?

Maybe not. What if that site was some kind of trap where lots of dinosaurs died over the centuries, like a tar bed? Or maybe that *Allosaurus* group was driven together by a drought or flood or something.

It's an argument that might not get settled until we have better fossil evidence, or a time machine.

FAILURE TO LUNCH

So how did herbivores survive in a world full of monsters like *Tyrannosaurus* and *Utahraptor*? Answer: *very carefully!*

From looking at their leg bones, we think that the big sauropods couldn't run at all. But—luckily for them—they were probably too big to be a meal for most predators. *Tyrannosaurus* would take one look and keep going.

But other herbivores—even bulldozer-size ones such as ten-ton *Triceratops*—were fair game. To survive, these dinosaurs had to evolve some nifty defenses.

DEFENSE! (BOOM, BOOM.) DEFENSE!

C-A-M-O-U-F-L-A-G-E! Many dinosaurs probably had patterned scales or feathers to blend into their surroundings.

M-U-S-C-L-E-S! Big ceratopsian dinosaurs were built like a modern-day rhino—muscular in the front but wimpy in the back. This way they could charge at attackers like a battering ram.

S-P-E-E-D! Duck-billed hadrosaurs looked like sitting ducks for carnivores, but they're the most common dinosaur specimens around. Paleontologists think that they used superior endurance to outrun their enemies.

S-P-I-K-E-S! Many dinosaurs tried to scare off hungry predators by looking very, very pointy. There's a classic *The Far Side* cartoon about a *Stegosaurus* that used its tail spikes to take out a caveman called Thag. Scientists now call these spikes the "thagomizer"! *Stegosaurus* must have had a very effective thagomizer, as we've found an *Allosaurus* fossil with a *Stegosaurus*-spike-size hole in its tailbone.

N-O-I-S-E! Lots of dinosaurs had spikes, but none were weirder than *Amargasaurus*'s double row of tall spines running all the way down its back. One scientist has suggested that *Amargasaurus* could knock its spines together like a rattle, to scare away enemies.

H-O-R-N-S! We've found a *Triceratops* skeleton with its nose horn snapped clean off. Even if their horns and frills were mostly decorative, they might have come in handy in combat as well.

DE-FENSE

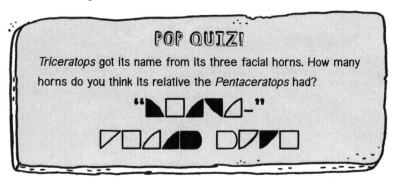

POP QUIZ!

Triceratops got its name from its three facial horns. How many horns do you think its relative the *Pentaceratops* had?

"◼◣◥◿–"
▽◻◿◢ ◰▽▷◻

THICK-SKINNED

The most successful dinosaurs protected themselves from predators with an amazing variety of body armor. Let's see what the well-dressed dinosaur is wearing this season!

Scutellosaurus is sporting more than three hundred bony bumps, each smaller than a bottle cap, built into its skin.

Ankylosaurus is covered in fused plates of armor so hard that they could withstand a *Tyrannosaurus* bite. And watch out for that giant wrecking ball on the tail! It's shattered many a *T. rex* shinbone.

Sauropelta is just as tanklike as *Ankylosaurus*, but with a little extra flair. Get a load of those neck spikes!

Gastonia is a walking fortress in this impressive getup—a thick bony skull, plates under its skin, spikes all over its neck and sides, and a double row on the tail. It's a breathtaking look from any angle!

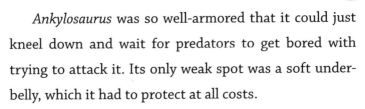

Euoplocephalus has armored shutters on its eyelids!

Ankylosaurus was so well-armored that it could just kneel down and wait for predators to get bored with trying to attack it. Its only weak spot was a soft underbelly, which it had to protect at all costs.

All that armor had a downside, though. It was *heavy*. Most *Ankylosaurus* fossils are discovered upside-down. These dinosaurs were probably flipped onto their backs by a river or mudslide and couldn't get back onto their feet.

Speaking of which, I need you to get onto *your* feet, Junior Geniuses. It's time to line up for lunch!

LUNCH

From what you've learned in today's lessons, you might have the idea that there were two basic kinds of dinosaurs—gentle, tree-grazing herbivores, and snarling, razor-clawed carnivores. In fact, that's what paleontologists thought for many years as well. But we now think that the truth about dino diets is a little more complicated.

WHAT?! Some dinosaurs were *omnivores*—they ate meat *and* vegetation. Some were *insectivores* who ate bugs. *Oviraptor* had no teeth at all, but it still preyed on little lizards. Some scary-looking dinosaurs were scavengers who picked carcasses clean but would never have started a fight.

Baryonyx had a giant hook for a claw and 128 teeth, twice as many as most other theropods. But from its long, weak jaw and the fossilized fish scales we've found in its innards, we know that *Baryonyx* was no bloodthirsty

beast. It probably fed on all fours by leaning over a river and scooping out fish with its long claw, the same way a grizzly bear might today.

Therizinosaurus was a theropod with three-foot swordlike claws on each hand! (Don't worry; it was mostly an herbivore. It probably used its ninja claws to dig into termite mounds for bugs or to strip bark off trees.) Its cousin *Deinocheirus* has a name meaning "horrible hand" because of its razor-sharp talons and eight-foot arms, the longest arms of any upright dinosaur! (But we now know it was a gentle giant who just used its long reach to gather vegetation or scoop up tiny fish from rivers.)

If there's one food that I bet all dinosaurs could agree on, it would be cookies.

Everyone likes cookies! Normally fossils take thousands of years to form, but if you're hungry now, here's a recipe that will help you and a grown-up get some fossils made in less than an hour.

FOSSIL COOKIES 🐾 ────────

INGREDIENTS

1 cup butter, softened

1 cup sugar

1 egg

1 tablespoon milk

1 teaspoon vanilla

3 cups flour

1/4 teaspoon salt

Plastic toys to "fossilize"

Directions

1. Cream the butter and sugar together, and then beat in the egg, milk, and vanilla.

2. Mix the flour and salt together separately. Add slowly to the wet ingredients. (Break out the electric mixer if you're not worried about using post-Jurassic technologies! But you probably want to smooth it all together with a wooden spoon afterward, because the dough will be as dry as a Colorado fossil bed.)

3. Divide the dough into two balls and roll each one out until it's between 1/4-inch and 1/2-inch thick. (Dusting the rolling pin and rolling surface with flour or powdered

sugar will help. But rolling the dough between two sheets of waxed paper makes the rolling even easier.)

4. Preheat your oven to 375°.

5. Use a knife or pizza cutter to divide the dough into squarish pieces, two to three inches on a side.

6. Into each cookie, press the shape you want to fossilize. Some ideas: seashells; little toy dinosaurs; plastic creepy-crawlies, such as spiders or centipedes; or footprints from other toys. Make sure each toy is washed clean first! You don't want your cookies to lead to a mass extinction event.

7. Transfer the squares to a cookie sheet and bake about 7 to 12 minutes. About halfway through, remove the baking sheet and re-press each cookie for a better fossil imprint. Rotate the cookie sheet and put it back into the oven. You'll know the fossil cookies are done when they just start to brown around the edges.

8. Study your fossils for years in a lab, trying to find out all you can about the strange creatures who left these imprints. Just kidding! As soon as the "fossils" are cool, eat as many as you can before a grown-up notices you're spoiling your dinner. Remind them that these are *educational* treats!

FIFTH PERIOD

REPTILES HIGH AND LOW

During the late Triassic period, there was no getting away from giant reptile monsters. Sure, they were crawling all over the land. But that was just the beginning. The skies and oceans were full of reptiles as well.

But be careful, Junior Geniuses! These reptiles were *not* dinosaurs. They evolved separately from the ornithischians and saurischians. But  they were just as amazing as any dinosaur—and, luckily for us, they are just as extinct.

IT'S A BIRD! IT'S A PLANE!

It's common to call winged Mesozoic reptiles "pterodactyls," but as a Junior Genius, you should know that this is *ptotally* the wrong *pterm*. These flying reptiles were called pterosaurs. Pterodactyl was just one specific *ptype* of pterosaur.

Pterosaur bodies were uniquely adapted to life in the friendly skies.

Air-filled bones. Pterosaur bones were full of tiny pockets lined with air sacs and connected to the lungs. You could say that pterosaurs breathed with their whole skeletons!

Hair! Yup, at the same time dinosaurs were developing feathers, flying reptiles were growing hair! Pterosaurs were covered with little fuzzy fibers similar to the hair on your head.

A tail rudder. *Rhamphorhynchus* was a pterosaur with a diamond-shaped vane at the end of its tail, which it might have used to stabilize itself or to steer.

A nose fin for tight turns. Why did so many pterosaurs have a fancy head crest? Some scientists think it was aerodynamic, a fin to help them make quick course changes while soaring after prey.

UGLY DUCKLINGS

Not all pterosaurs had the awesome pointy head crest you are picturing. That was *Pteranodon*, and it looked pretty cool. But check out its weird-looking cousins.

Pteranodon:
pointy head crest

Dimorphodon:
head shaped
like a puffin's

Dsungaripterus:
weird nose

Pterodaustro:
goofy smile

POP QUIZ!

Pterodaustro used its wide "tooth comb" to strain food out of shallow waters. The reddish brine shrimp it ate might even have turned its skin pink! Do you know what modern animal gets its pink color from the tiny shrimp it eats?

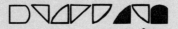

Of course, a pterosaur's most important adaptation was its wings. Let's take a closer look:

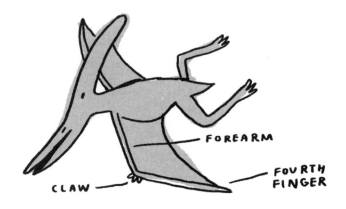

As you can see, most of the length of each wing was a leathery flap connected to one insanely long finger. That's right. Pterosaur wings were really just their fourth finger, specially adapted. The biggest pterosaurs had a fourth finger taller than any human!

Can you imagine life with one eight-foot finger on each hand? Scratching your back would be so easy, but picking your nose might be dangerous.

TERROR SOARS

Pterosaurs came in all shapes and sizes, some as small as the sparrow-size *Nemicolopterus*, discovered in China in 2008. But let's get down to it. You want to know what the biggest ones were, right? Meet the *azhdarchids*.

From their weird name, the azhdarchids probably sound like some kind of terrible nightmare dragon from a fantasy book, but— Wait. Actually, that's exactly what they were.

Azhdarchids had incredible long necks and legs, so the biggest ones, such as *Quetzalcoatlus* and *Hatzegopteryx*, were roughly the size and shape of giraffes.

HOMEWORK

"*Quetzalcoatlus*" and "*Hatzegopteryx*" are very hard words to say, but at least they are worth lots and lots of points in Scrabble! If you have a Scrabble set handy, can you figure out which pterosaur is a higher-scoring word? Are there any dinosaur names that are worth even *more* points?

So imagine a giraffe with a ten-foot beak, big enough to swallow you whole. *Quetzalcoatlus* had a *much* larger head than any theropod.

And remember that *Quetzalcoatlus* also had a thirty-five-foot wingspan. That's wider than most small aircraft.

GULP!

We know from looking at their footprints that pterosaurs were pretty clumsy on land, where they walked on all fours. But in the air they were incredibly graceful. *Quetzalcoatlus* was so big that it would have needed a cliff or a hillside to get up to takeoff velocity, but once in the air, it rarely needed to flap its wings for very long. Pterosaurs were mostly gliders, soaring through the sky at speeds of up to eighty miles per hour by riding updrafts of warm air.

Because the flight of azhdarchids was so efficient, scientists have calculated that big azhdarchids could have handled trips of more than ten thousand miles—nonstop!

EXTRA CREDIT

The longest commercial flight operating today is a seventeen-hour nonstop between Dallas, Texas, and Sydney, Australia. That's 8,578 miles. So *Quetzalcoatlus* might very well have flown across continents and even oceans with its amazing wings. It was the master of the world!

FISH STORY

As you'll remember, it took animals hundreds of millions of years to evolve legs and walk out of the ocean. But around the start of the Triassic period, some reptiles decided they were through living on land, and they wandered back into the waves. Today turtles are the only reptiles that live in the sea. But during the Mesozoic, the seas were full of giant reptiles.

There were giants in the deep sea hundreds of millions of years before the dinosaurs, of course. The Devonian period is called the Age of Fishes because of the thousands of weird fish that began to take over the seas about 400 million years ago. At the top of the Devonian food chain was the *Dunkleosteus*, a heavily armored fish the size of an elephant. Its tough outer scales were covered in dentin and enamel—and, because you evolved from prehistoric fish like these, you still have a set of those dentin-and-enamel scales today. We call them . . . "teeth"!

Another order of Devonian fish, the coelacanths, was well-known to scientists through fossils but was

believed to have gone extinct with the dinosaurs. Then one day in December 1938, a South African museum curator named Marjorie Courtenay-Latimer decided to visit the city dock, so she could wish a fisherman friend a merry Christmas. There on the deck of his ship, she saw, she later wrote, "the most beautiful fish I had ever seen." She hauled the five-foot fish into a taxicab, much to the driver's annoyance, and took it back to her museum. A few weeks later she discovered that the fish was a species

 of coelacanth, still living in the Indian Ocean after all these years!

When the age of dinosaurs began, the oceans were ruled by sharks—but really weird ones. So weird that you're going to think I'm making them up. But I'm not.

For example, *Helicoprion* had more than a hundred teeth in its lower jaw, just like sharks today. But *Helicoprion*'s teeth were arranged in a spiral whorl, sort of like the teeth on a circular saw blade! I have *no idea* how it chewed.

Stethacanthus had teeth in an even weirder place—on its back! Its anvil-shaped fin was covered with tiny teeth scales called *denticles*, which it might have used to hitch a ride on the belly of larger neighbors when it got tired of swimming.

HEAVYWEIGHT CHOMP

The scariest shark in the prehistoric ocean lived millions of years *after* the dinosaurs. *Megalodon*'s name means "mighty tooth"—and it's not hard to see why. This giant shark had forty-six razor-sharp teeth, each one the size of this book. Its jaw could slam shut with a force of up to eighteen tons. That's thirty times stronger than a lion's jaw. And what did *Megalodon* eat with those big bites? *Anything it wanted.*

SEA MONSTERS

The first large reptiles to return to the ocean were the sleek, streamlined ichthyosaurs—"fish lizards." Imagine a reptile about the size and shape of a dolphin, but not nearly as cute.

SIGH...

EVOLUTION TIPS WITH
MR. CHARLES DARWIN

Dolphins, of course, aren't fish *or* lizards. They're mammals.
Ichthyosaurs aren't dolphin-shaped because they're related to
dolphins, but just because they adapted separately to the same
environment. Hey, they didn't do it on "porpoise"! HA, HA, HA!

DARWIN

Ichthyosaurs beat their powerful tails from side
to side like a shark, and could swim at speeds of up to
twenty-five miles per hour. They were excellent hunters,
thanks to huge, sensitive ear bones and keen eyes.
Ophthalmosaurus had eyes the size of grapefruits that
pretty much took up its whole skull.

It probably used those giant eyes to hunt in the blackness of deep ocean waters, so we know that ichthyosaurs must have been pretty good at holding their breath. That's right. All these ocean reptiles of the dinosaur age had lungs, not gills. Just like modern whales, they'd have to surface every time they needed to breathe.

We have some amazing snapshots of ichthyosaur life, thanks to famous fossils from around the world.

GERMANY! Mesozoic marine reptiles didn't lay eggs. They all gave birth to live young. How do we know? From fossils found in Germany of a baby ichthyosaur, emerging from its mother, tail-first.

NEVADA! In 1928, a weird geometric arrangement of ichthyosaur bones was discovered in Nevada. It's controversial, but one scientist has theorized that the bones were placed in that pattern by a giant creature who hunted ichthyosaurs, maybe even an intelligent giant octopus using the bones of its prey to make a

self-portrait of its own tentacles! This mystery monster has been named the Triassic Kraken.

ENGLAND! Ichthyosaurs ate fish and squid-like creatures called belemnites. In 2002, a British paleontologist found a fossil of undigested belemnite shells. An ichthyosaur must have thrown up the shells. It's fossilized barf!

GROSS!

JUNIOR GENIUS
VOCABULARY BOOSTER

If you want to sound smart around paleontologists, don't say "barf." There's a word for fossilized puddles of vomit. They're called *regurgitalites*!

THE NECKS BIG THING

Ichthyosaurs ruled the Mesozoic seas for millions of years before being replaced by another kind of giant reptile, plesiosaurs. Plesiosaurs aren't dinosaurs, but they're cool because they look *exactly* how you'd think a prehistoric sea reptile should look.

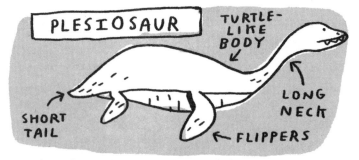

The plesiosaurs are descended from nothosaurs, Triassic reptiles that fished at sea but rested on land, like seals do. Eventually they moved into the water full-time. Scientists used to think that plesiosaurs swam by rowing their flippers like oars on a boat. Now we think they flapped them up and down, "flying" through the water like a penguin.

Another suborder of plesiosaurs had much shorter necks—and shorter tempers. The pliosaurs were ferocious whale-size predators that liked to snack on other plesiosaurs. *Liopleurodon*'s skull was longer than a compact car and was lined with spiky teeth. *Kronosaurus*, the largest, was more than thirty feet long and had a stronger bite than a *Tyrannosaurus*.

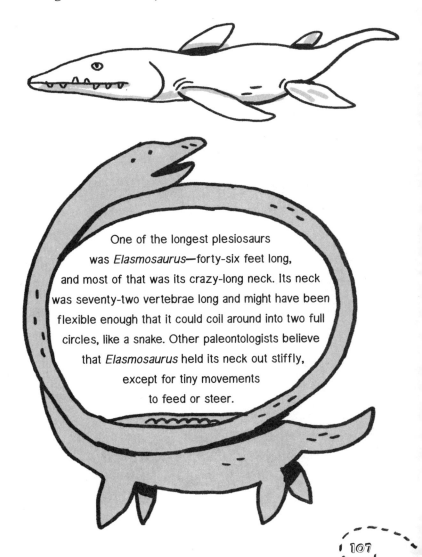

One of the longest plesiosaurs was *Elasmosaurus*—forty-six feet long, and most of that was its crazy-long neck. Its neck was seventy-two vertebrae long and might have been flexible enough that it could coil around into two full circles, like a snake. Other paleontologists believe that *Elasmosaurus* held its neck out stiffly, except for tiny movements to feed or steer.

END OF AN ERA

In the Cretaceous period, the plesiosaurs were replaced by even bigger, scarier predators, the mosasaurs. We once thought that the mosasaurs were slow swimmers, wiggling through the water like eels, but new fossils found in 2008 reveal the imprints of a sharklike tail. These killing machines actually cruised through the Cretaceous oceans at speeds around thirty miles per hour, eating everything in their paths. We've found entire birds, sharks, fish, and other mosasaurs in their fossil remains, so we know they swallowed their prey whole.

Yes, the seas back then were full of wonders, Junior Geniuses.

Soft-shelled turtles the size of Volkswagens.

ARCHELON

Crocodiles that roamed the open ocean.

TELEOSAURUS

Fish the length of a volleyball court.

LEEDSICHTHYS

And then they all disappeared. The dinosaurs, the flying pterosaurs, and the plesiosaurs and mosasaurs in the ocean. All extinct after ruling the earth for millions of years, all forgotten except for their fossilized bones. Where did they go? What happened?

That's what we're about to find out . . . after a quick break for music class.

One dinosaur mystery that we will probably never solve is this: What kind of noises did they make? Sadly, there were no tape recorders or microphones 100 million years ago.

In movies, of course, dinosaurs roar and bellow. The sound engineers in *Jurassic Park* combined dozens of different noises to get the right effects. These sounds included:

geese hissing

alligators grunting

a baby elephant trumpeting

dolphins squeaking

whales blowing air

even the sound designer's pet terrier tugging on a rope!

The grunting of the movie's killer *T. rex* came from a much cuter source in real life—a koala bear!

I don't want you to be too disappointed, but it's at least possible that dinosaurs made no noise at all. Modern reptiles make sounds using an organ called a *larynx*, just like you and I do, but birds have a totally different system. Their tweeter is called a *syrinx*. If those systems evolved independently, then maybe their common ancestor, prehistoric reptiles, were totally silent.

But most scientists, looking at the shape of dinosaur skulls, think that the skulls were designed to amplify noise. Forest-dwelling dinosaurs might have made high-pitched sounds, which would have carried better through the trees. One scientist, studying a *Tyrannosaurus* skull, decided that it might actually have croaked like a frog, rather than roaring like a lion.

RIBBIT!

The dinosaur we think might have been the most musical was *Parasaurolophus*. Its weird crest was once thought to be a snorkel for underwater breathing. Today we think there were airways in the crest that *Parasaurolophus* could use to make a low-frequency musical noise, the same way whales and elephants communicate. Some scientists built a version of the crest using plastic piping, and they think they've duplicated *Parasaurolophus*'s call—a low, rumbly B-flat!

The next time you see a piano, play the lowest B-flat on the keyboard. I don't think you'll attract any *Parasaurolophus*, but it's worth a shot.

UH-OH!

SIXTH PERIOD

STOP! MAMMAL TIME

Dinosaurs—have you seen one lately? Go over to the window. Count the dinosaurs. A lot of them were really big, right? They'd be hard to miss.

I'm just having a little fun with you, Junior Geniuses. As you know, none of us will ever see a living dinosaur. That's what "extinct" means—completely wiped out. And it's not just the dinosaurs. According to some estimates, 99.9 percent of all the species that have ever lived on earth are now extinct. We're the one-in-a-thousand form of life that's still around. High five!

Extinctions still happen in modern times. In the 1800s, the passenger pigeon was the most common bird in the world. There were up to five billion of them.

One in every three birds in America was a passenger pigeon! Then, in less than a century, they were gone. Like, not just rare but completely gone. The last known passenger pigeon, Martha, died in the Cincinnati Zoo in 1914. That's what extinction looks like. One day there are billions of your kind. Then, in the blink of an evolutionary eye, you're gone.

In the case of the passenger pigeon, we know what killed them—humans cutting down the trees they needed to build nests, and hunting them for food because they tasted so good.

GOING . . . GOING . . .

Could we be in the middle of another mass extinction right now, the first one since the dinosaurs died? Biologists worry that animal populations are dropping fast, from lions to frogs to sharks to rhinos. The World Wildlife Fund estimates that the wildlife population of earth has been cut in half just in the last forty years!

I want you Junior Geniuses to live in a world with lions and sharks. (Not so you get eaten. I just think they are cool animals.) So we need to get serious about conservation, before some of our favorite species are gone forever.

IT CAME FROM OUTER SPACE!

Humans didn't kill the dinosaurs. We have a pretty good alibi. We were sixty million years away from existing when everything went down.

For decades scientists argued over why all the dinosaurs died so suddenly, all over the world. The theories were all over the place.

In 1962, one scientist wrote a paper blaming a new suspect for killing the dinosaurs—butterflies! He

wondered if the world's first butterflies ate too many leaves when they were in caterpillar form, which killed off vegetation that dinosaurs needed to survive. Hmm ... a caterpillar vs. *Argentinosaurus*. Who would win?

But today we're pretty sure who killed the dinosaurs.

In 1980, a team of scientists found that a layer of rock from 66 million years ago—the same time when the dinosaurs disappeared—was loaded with an element called iridium. This was an important clue. Iridium is rare on earth but much more common in meteorites. There was also lots of ash and soot in the same rock layer—all over the world. In other words, signs of the biggest forest fire of all time.

Here's what must have happened: Something big, such as an asteroid or comet, smashed into the earth. If it was an asteroid, it might have been about the size of a small moon. If it was a comet, it was traveling at up to one hundred thousand miles per hour! Either way, this is what happened next:

Something big and hard tore a one-hundred-mile-wide hole in the earth. We've found the crater, just off the coast of Mexico. At the end of the Cretaceous period, that was a shallow sea. When we drill down into the crater today, we find a layer of melted rock. That's what you'd expect from an explosion as powerful as two hundred *million* atomic bombs.

OUT OF THIS WORLD

The impact was so powerful that the rocks it kicked up could have shot out into space, sending little chunks of the earth all the way to Mars or the moons of Jupiter! We may find them there someday.

WIPEOUT

Here's what happens when a rock the size of Manhattan slams into the earth.

WARNING: NOT MUCH OF IT IS GOOD NEWS.

1. The explosion instantly vaporizes everything in a six-hundred-mile circle. The ocean boils. Imagine, one second, you're a happy hadrosaur thinking, *Hey, what's that big falling thing?* The next, you're a cloud of hot dust.

2. Creatures hundreds of miles away are blinded by the flash of the impact.

3. A hot blast wave rushes outward at the speed of sound, frying every creature in its path.

4. The shock wave keeps circling the globe. It's so loud, it can deafen dinosaurs a continent away from the crater.

5. The splash creates a mega-tsunami, and a wall of water a mile high (!) floods coastal areas.

6. Earthquakes and volcanoes are triggered, eventually spreading all over the world.

7. Sand and rock kicked into the atmosphere by the initial impact begin to fall again. As it descends through the atmosphere, it heats up into tiny white-hot spheres of glass. This deadly rain pours down, causing massive wildfires. Within two hours, anything outside is dead.

8. A massive mushroom cloud of dust rises into the atmosphere, blocking out the sun for up to year. Rain turns to acid.

Any *one* of those things would be bad enough. I don't know about you, but one molten-glass shower is enough to ruin my whole day! All eight disasters at once—well, the dinosaurs didn't stand a chance.

When the dust had settled (literally!), no land animal larger than a dog was left in the entire world. Flowering plants were nearly wiped out.

Three quarters of all species on earth were gone, never to be seen again.

SOLE SURVIVORS

Remember how I said that *Microraptor* and its cousins were the smallest dinosaurs? I have a confession to make. That's not technically true. Modern birds are so closely related to dinosaurs that most scientists still classify them as part of Maniraptora, a subgroup of theropod dinosaurs! Maniraptora are dinosaurs that got smaller and grew thicker feathers and survived the mass extinction. If we count today's ten thousand species of birds as dinosaurs, then the smallest dinosaur ever to live is probably the two-inch-long Cuban bee hummingbird, which is still around today!

I guess I was wrong when I said earlier that you couldn't see dinosaurs out your window. You just needed to look up.

THE STORY OF US

I know that last part was pretty sad, Junior Geniuses, with all the dinosaurs dying in increasingly horrible ways. But dry your tears! There is a silver lining to this cloud of thick meteor dust. And that silver lining is humans! Without the mass extinction of the dinosaurs, the evolution of mammals would have been very different. If not for the giant space fireball, *you would not even exist*!

Mammals evolved side by side with the dinosaurs, but the early mammals were very small. One of the first, called *Hadrocodium*, was about the size of a paper clip. Like other early mammals, it laid eggs!

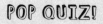

POP QUIZ!

This isn't as weird as it sounds. What duck-billed Australian mammal still lays eggs today?

Over a span of millions of years, mammals got bigger. The fossil of one feisty beaver-size mammal, *Repenomamus*, was found in China with bones of a baby *Psittacosaurus* dinosaur preserved in its stomach. So some mammals even ate dinosaurs.

The mass extinction of giant reptiles ended the Mesozoic era and began a new geologic time frame, the Cenozoic era. If you want to see the Cenozoic era up close, just go outside and go for a walk. We still live in the Cenozoic today.

CENOZOIC ERA

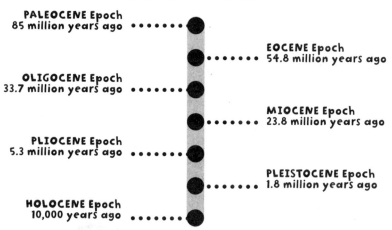

PALEOCENE Epoch
85 million years ago

EOCENE Epoch
54.8 million years ago

OLIGOCENE Epoch
33.7 million years ago

MIOCENE Epoch
23.8 million years ago

PLIOCENE Epoch
5.3 million years ago

PLEISTOCENE Epoch
1.8 million years ago

HOLOCENE Epoch
10,000 years ago

In the Cenozoic era, without giant monsters such as *Tyrannosaurus* around, mammals were finally at the top of the food chain! The variety of different kinds of mammals exploded, with evolution mixing and matching combinations you would not believe. Let's do some Miocene math.[3]

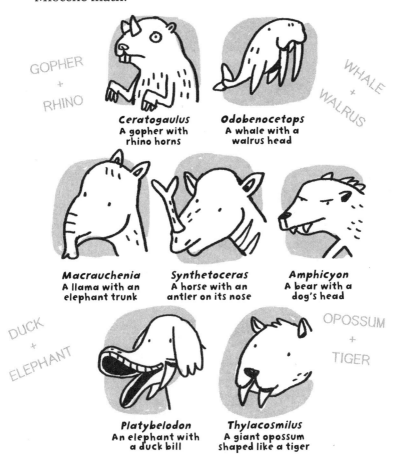

GOPHER + RHINO

WHALE + WALRUS

Ceratogaulus
A gopher with rhino horns

Odobenocetops
A whale with a walrus head

Macrauchenia
A llama with an elephant trunk

Synthetoceras
A horse with an antler on its nose

Amphicyon
A bear with a dog's head

DUCK + ELEPHANT

OPOSSUM + TIGER

Platybelodon
An elephant with a duck bill

Thylacosmilus
A giant opossum shaped like a tiger

[3] Okay, some of these mammals actually lived during the Eocene or Oligocene epochs. But "Miocene math" sounds better.

EXTRA CREDIT

Thylacosmilus's enormous fangs kept growing its entire life. It had to grind them short against its lower teeth to keep from stabbing itself in the mouth! This also kept them nice and sharp.

So nature had a lot of bad ideas, is what I'm saying. But the freakiest combination of all, in my well-informed opinion, didn't appear until the Pliocene epoch. *Chalicotherium* was a sort of upside-down centaur. It had a horse head, but it walked on its knuckles like a gorilla. Horse-apes! That's a fun thing to have nightmares about for years!

OLD GROWTH

Some prehistoric mammals looked like scaled-down versions of more familiar animals, like those mini candy bars you get on Halloween.

"FUN" SIZE

CHOCO BAR MINI

WAY MORE FUN SIZE →

CHOCO BAR

For example, the first horses were the size of dogs, and the first elephant-like creatures were smaller than pigs. *Leptomeryx* was a deer as small—and as fast—as a rabbit. Awww.

But lots of extinct mammals were big. *Really* big. Scientists call these animals "ridiculously oversize creatures you'd never want to meet in real life." Wait, no, that's a little long. They're called *megafauna*.

Most of these mammals thrived during the Pleistocene epoch, a couple million years ago. Back then there were literally . . .

- **Armadillos the size of Volkswagens**

- **Elk with twelve-foot antlers**

- **Kangaroos as big as bears**

- **Saber-toothed tigers that could open their mouths twice as wide as a lion**

- **Beavers as tall as a human**

- **Sloths bigger than elephants**

GULP!

The biggest land mammal of all time was the *Paraceratherium*, which wandered central Asia during the Oligocene epoch munching on treetop leaves. Imagine a hornless rhino the height of a giraffe, and you'll be pretty close. (But don't get too close.)

LAST OF THE GIANTS

Paraceratherium's later cousin, *Elasmotherium*, had an enormous six-foot horn on its head. Imagine, a giant rhinoceros whose horn *alone* is taller than a person! Siberian tribes told stories about a giant "unicorn" that lived out on the snow. They might have been remembering *Elasmotherium*.

Isn't it weird that early man lived at the same time as some of this extinct megafauna? One tiny population of mammoths survived the Ice Age and was still living on Siberia's Wrangel Island as late as 1650 BC, one thousand years *after* Stonehenge and the Egyptian pyramids were built. There were still giant cattle called aurochs wandering the forests of Poland in 1620, when the Pilgrims landed at Plymouth Rock. And we actually have movie footage of the thylacine, a wolflike marsupial that roamed Australia 4 million years ago. The last one died in Tasmania in 1936.

FROZEN

The Pleistocene epoch, the age of megafauna, was also earth's last major ice age. Two-mile-thick ice sheets covered ten million square miles of the earth. So much water was frozen that sea levels dropped like crazy. You could walk from England to France, or from Alaska to Russia.

Animals have always migrated in response to climate changes. About 120,000 years ago, for example, England was warm enough for hippos to live there! But an icy world was a playground for big, furry megafauna, well-insulated from the cold. Woolly mammoths and rhinos wandered the tundra in vast herds. One cave in Austria contains the remains of more than thirty thousand cave bears! (That's not the result of one massive cave bear accident. The bones accumulated there over thousands of years.)

BABY, IT'S COLD OUTSIDE

Dinosaur remains are just fossils, but scientists sometimes find whole mammoth carcasses intact, frozen in ice or soil. In 2007, a reindeer breeder in Russia discovered a female mammoth calf so well preserved that she still has fur and there's still milk in her stomach! An autopsy revealed—forty-two thousand years too late!—that she died by sinking into the mud as her herd crossed a river. Baby Lyuba, as scientists named her, has toured museums on three continents.

Giant animals like the mammoths may have gone extinct due to hunting from the first modern humans. We've found remains of villages in eastern Europe where prehistoric people built houses out of mammoth bones and tusks instead of logs. Don't mess with those guys!

KINGS OF THE STONE AGE

About 20 million years ago apes evolved from monkeys, and 3 million years ago some of them began to walk upright. We're not sure why they stood up, but it actually happened long before brain size began to grow. If you ever watch reality TV, maybe you're not surprised that there were primates who could stand upright but whose brains weren't very advanced.

The scientific name for the human species is *Homo sapiens*. "*Homo*" means "human," and "*sapiens*" means "wise," in honor of our big, big brains. But lots of other *hominid* (humanlike) species lived and died in the time it took us to evolve.

GIGANTOPITHECUS. If you want one hominid on your basketball team, it's this one. Our biggest ancestor, *Gigantopithecus* was ten feet tall and weighed as much as three gorillas. *Gigantopithecus* survived for nine million years and went extinct only 100,000 years ago. (Unless they survived and are bigfoot.)

AUSTRALOPITHECUS. These primates looked more humanlike than any other hominid around 3 or 4 million years ago. The most famous *Australopithecus* skeleton, discovered in Ethiopia in 1974, was a female that scientists named Lucy. Why? They were listening to "Lucy in the Sky with Diamonds" by the Beatles when they found her.

HOMO FLORESIENSIS. These folks, whose bones were discovered recently in Indonesia, have been called hobbits. Even fully grown, they were all probably shorter than you—3.5 feet tall, on average. These hobbits had chimpanzee-size brains, so they probably wouldn't have survived a long journey to Mordor.

NEANDERTHALS. These close cousins of *Homo sapiens* died out around 40,000 years ago. Did they disappear when they interbred with humans, or when we killed them off? Did they die from the cold? We don't know. But there are new archaeological clues that Neanderthals were more advanced than you might guess. They probably had a simple spoken language. They buried their dead and may even have left flowers by the graves!

JUNIOR GENIUS JOVIALITY

Q: What did the caveman like to do on weekends?
A: Go clubbing!

We are the only species left in genus *Homo*, the ones who survived. That's mostly because of the cool technology we came up with over the years. *Gigantopithecus* may have been good at reaching tall things, but it wasn't much of an inventor. Humans, on the other hand, have been on a roll lately.

1.8 million years ago—Fire

500,000 years ago—Houses

400,000 years ago—Spears

16,000 years ago—Pottery

5,500 years ago—The wheel

2,200 years ago—Paper

40 years ago—Video games

Who knows what we'll come up with next? Hopefully jet packs, because that would be amazing.

SEVENTH PERIOD

BONEHEADS

Today any library will have a whole section on prehistoric creatures. We know shelves-full of facts about them—a few of which I've tried to fill you with today, Junior Geniuses. But can you imagine living in a world that had no idea what dinosaurs even were? It's hard to believe that until two centuries ago, the word "dinosaur" didn't even exist.

I HAVE NO IDEA WHAT A "DINOSAUR" IS.

GEORGE WASHINGTON

JA, WHAT A FUNNY WORD!

MOZART

That's right. Dinosaurs roamed the earth for more than 150 million years—but for almost all of human history, we had absolutely no idea they existed!

Which is weird, because people had been digging up fossils for thousands of years.

CHINA! Two thousand years ago dinosaur fossils were thought to be the bones, teeth, and horns of dragons. People would grind them up to make medicine.

GREECE! The legendary griffin from Greek myth—half lion, half eagle—may have originated with beaked *Protoceratops* skulls found by gold miners in Asia.

AMERICA! The Sioux people found bones from *Megacerops*, a rhino-like Eocene mammal, and thought they were the mythical "thunder horses" whose wild stampedes in the sky explained thunderstorms.

These are all great stories, but we never would have known the truth about prehistoric life without the hard work and amazing brains of a new kind of scientist—paleontologists!

Let's finish our prehistoric journey by jumping forward in time millions of years to see how new discoveries are being made every day by dinosaur detectives.

DINO-MANIA!

This is the dinosaur bone that changed everything.

A British professor named Robert Plot dug it up near Oxford in 1676 and, puzzled by its size, wrote an article on it. He thought it might have been the thighbone of an elephant brought to England by the ancient Romans, or even from one of the giants mentioned in the biblical book of Genesis.

Surprise! *It was not either of those things!* Over the next century other scientists began finding more giant

bones and realized they were from extinct reptiles. In 1824, Plot's historic fossil was renamed *Megalosaurus* ("great lizard"), making it the first dinosaur ever named.

EXTRA CREDIT

Robert Plot's fossil has been lost, which is a real shame. We now know that *Megalosaurus* remains are very hard to come by. The first dinosaur fossil ever studied was, through a weird coincidence, a very, very rare one!

Two decades later a biologist named Richard Owen used *Megalosaurus* and two other specimens to define a new kind of reptile that he called Dinosauria, from the Greek for "terrible lizard."

We now know that dinosaurs aren't lizards, and most of them weren't terrible at all but were quite nice, in fact. But the name stuck. All of a sudden Victorian England had dinosaur fever. Giant dinosaurs were sculpted and placed outside the Crystal Palace in London. Charles Dickens even included a shout-out to *Megalosaurus* in the first paragraph of his greatest novel, *Bleak House*.

It was just like nowadays, when a popular dinosaur movie comes out and all the fast-food kid meals have dinosaur toys. Only, more old-timey.

ROCK STARS

Thanks to the dinosaur boom, discoveries began to explode from a new kind of celebrity, the dinosaur hunters. Here are a few of the great early paleontologists.

THE ADVENTURER! American explorer **ROY CHAPMAN ANDREWS** discovered that the Gobi Desert of Mongolia was a treasure trove of dinosaur bones. His team braved bandits, sandstorms, and blizzards to discover the first *Protoceratops* and *Velociraptor* bones, as well as the first fossils of dinosaur

eggs. Because of his globe-trotting adventures, broad-brimmed hat, and fear of snakes, many believe that Andrews was the model for the movie hero Indiana Jones.

THE SPY! **BARNUM BROWN,** the discoverer of *Tyrannosaurus rex*, was also a one-of-a-kind globe-trotter. Nicknamed Mr. Bones, he roamed the world in an oversize fur coat,

digging for fossils while prospecting for oil—a clever way to get oil companies to pick up the tab for his adventures. During World War II, he went to work as an intelligence agent for the U.S. government, which wanted his knowledge from his years of traveling in Greece, Africa, India, and Burma.

THE SEASHELL SELLER!

Britain's greatest early fossil collector was not allowed to join the Geological Society of London—because she was a woman! **MARY ANNING** spent years on the English coast digging up ocean fossils. When she was just twelve years old, she found the first ich-

> I SELL SEASHELLS BY THE SEASHORE.

thyosaur skeleton ever identified, and later discovered the first plesiosaur bones among thousands of other fossils. She opened a shop called Anning's Fossil Depot, which is where the popular tongue twister "She sells seashells by the seashore" comes from.

And Mary Anning's paleontology work was just as dangerous as Roy Chapman Andrews's, in its way. Anning made her best discoveries by fossil-hunting in the winter rain, when fresh landslides would expose new specimens. In 1833, she was almost killed when a cliff collapsed above her.

THE ENEMIES! EDWARD COPE and **O. C. MARSH** were the leading American fossil hunters of their time, and they hated each other. They worked for competing museums, and in the 1880s they both had crews digging at the same Colorado fossil bed. Things got ugly. Their workers would throw rocks at one another, spy on and steal from one another, and even destroy fossils so the other team couldn't study them. These Bone Wars eventually left both men unhappy and broke, so let that be a lesson to you, Junior Geniuses. (On the other hand, their bitter feud did uncover 142 new dinosaurs. Let that part *not* be a lesson to you.)

BAD TO THE BONE

What about the worst paleontologist? My vote would be for Gerard Smets, a Belgian clergyman who in 1888 announced a new duck-billed dinosaur he called *Aachenosaurus*. (Maybe he just wanted to have the first dinosaur in the dictionary?) Another paleontologist quickly shot down Smets's theory. The *Aachenosaurus* "bones," he pointed out, were just pieces of petrified wood. Smets was so embarrassed that he abandoned science completely and never studied fossils again.

DIE HARD

What is a dinosaur fossil, anyway? A grown-up might tell you that it's a bone that's been "turned to stone," like petrified wood. Not exactly true, Junior Geniuses!

Fossils form when water seeps its way into the little hollow spaces in bones and other tissue. Groundwater has dissolved minerals in it, and these minerals strengthen the bone so that it doesn't get crushed. Some of the bone may decay and get replaced by harder minerals, but most of the original calcium and stuff that made up the bone stays in the fossil. So when you see a dinosaur bone in a museum (not one of the resin casts they put out when the actual bones are too fragile), you're actually seeing the same bone that was once inside a dinosaur!

This *mineralization* process works only if the organism got covered in dirt immediately after death. Otherwise the bones might be disturbed by erosion or scavengers and decompose without leaving a trace. This explains why dinosaur fossils are so rare. We have only the bones of animals that were swallowed up by a mud slide, or animals that died in the desert and quickly had sand blown over them. The odds are something like one in a million that a dinosaur carcass will get fossilized. Now you know why every new find is so exciting for paleontologists.

So dinosaur detectives sometimes have to make do without many clues. Even for an iconic dinosaur such as *Pachycephalosaurus*, we have only a single complete skull. Everything we know has to come from that hunk of bone. For many years all we had from *Troodon* was just one tooth!

NOBODY'S PERFECT

Because good fossil finds are so rare, there's a lot of guess-work involved in paleontology. Sometimes the guesses don't turn out to be right.

NOPE!

The discoverer of *Iguanodon* thought that its thumb spike went on its nose.

O. C. Marsh thought that *Stegosaurus*'s plates were flat, like shingles, and that it walked around on two legs!

NO!

Marsh's archenemy Edward Cope made an even worse mistake with *Elasmosaurus*. He put the head on the wrong end!

NOT EXACTLY!

So even your standard fossil is something pretty amazing—a bone that landed in exactly the right place to survive for millions of years. But some fossils are even weirder than that. Some fossils are . . .

RADIOACTIVE! When dinosaur bones get buried near deposits of minerals such as uranium, they produce radioactive fossils. On the plus side, these fossils are easier to find, because scientists can use a device called a Geiger counter to locate them. But the fossils sometimes have to be kept out of museums or covered in a layer of lead paint because of the dangerous radioactivity.

JEWELRY! Opals are some of the most valuable jewels in the world. In Australia, paleontologists have dug up fossils where the mineral that seeped into the original bone was opal. The result is dinosaur bones made out of precious gemstone.

POOP! Dinosaur droppings could fossilize as well. Scientists call these fossils *coprolites*, which is Greek for "poop rock." And dinosaurs sure could poop! One sample we have (from a *T. rex*, probably) is more than fifteen inches long—and that's just a fragment! Poop rock can be a treasure trove for scientists. If it contains fossilized

stems and seeds, we can tell exactly what that dinosaur used to eat. From its shape we can tell how the animal's intestines worked.

THE SWEET SMELL OF SUCCESS

In 2010, a Swiss company offered a luxury watch with a dial made of coprolites. The price tag for wearing a lump of dinosaur dung on your wrist? Just $11,290.

CAN YOU DIG IT?

Today dinosaur fossils have been found on all seven continents—including Antarctica, where the ice and cold make it *really* hard to dig.

Do you dream of being a dinosaur detective someday? Here's how fossils get from deep in the earth all the way to a science museum near you.

 **WARNING:** IT MIGHT BE MORE COMPLICATED THAN YOU THINK.

Find a fossil! Fossils are rare, but there are still a lot of them out there. From 1909 to 1924, scientists dug up 385 *tons* of fossils from Utah's Dinosaur National Monument. Today fossil hunters have more ways to look than ever. Some have tried radar to see under the earth's surface. Others have fired shotguns at the ground and used special microphones to detect the telltale echo of a buried dinosaur bone.

Chip away the surrounding rock. Shovels and even jackhammers can be used at first, but when you get close, what you need is real *CSI* stuff: chisels, brushes, and even those little picks your dentist uses. One false move could damage a priceless fossil. The first *Scelidosaurus* bones were found way back in 1858, but they didn't get dug up for more than a century because scientists couldn't figure out a safe way to get them out of their limestone bed! (The paleontologists finally used acid.)

Protect the fossil. You can't just put a few stamps on a fossil and throw it in the mail. Big bones have to be wrapped in plaster and burlap bandages to keep them safe on their way to the museum, a trick invented by Barnum Brown himself.

Lab work. Once the fossil is unpacked in the lab, that's when the real work begins. In some delicate cases, such as with dinosaur eggs, it may take a full year of work to chip into the fossil and reveal its secrets.

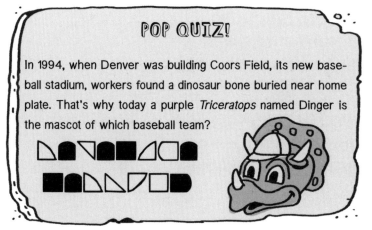

POP QUIZ!

In 1994, when Denver was building Coors Field, its new baseball stadium, workers found a dinosaur bone buried near home plate. That's why today a purple *Triceratops* named Dinger is the mascot of which baseball team?

See, dinosaur fossils aren't just for making casts to display in museums. They're full of clues that tell us what Mesozoic life was like. As we've seen, fossils can tell us what dinosaurs looked like, how they moved, and what they ate. By looking at the layer of rock the fossil came in—a science called *stratigraphy*—we can tell when the creature lived.

In rare cases the specimen will be in such good shape that we can see more than bone.

- *Edmontosaurus* remains are sometimes discovered "mummified," complete with fossilized skin.

- The first *Scipionyx* discovery had a fossilized windpipe and even red traces where its liver had been located.

- In 2005, paleontologist Mary Schweitzer made headlines when she discovered blood vessels and fossilized blood cells in a *Tyrannosaurus* bone.

BACK FROM THE DEAD

Do these traces of dinosaur cells mean that science is getting closer to cloning a live dinosaur, like in *Jurassic Park*? Unfortunately (or fortunately, if you remember how those movies turned out) that's probably not possible. In *Jurassic Park*, the prehistoric critters are cloned from dinosaur blood extracted from prehistoric mosquitoes trapped in fossilized amber. Now, it's true that amber is a great way for us to study ancient bugs. We have 230-million-year-old gnats from the Triassic period perfectly preserved, thanks to amber. But the problem is that no dinosaur DNA could survive that long. Studies on extinct birds show that DNA has a half-life of 521 years. That is, every 521 years, half of it decays. Even under perfect conditions, dinosaur DNA would be gone without a trace within 7 million years.

If you want to de-extinct-ify a prehistoric animal, mammoth carcasses trapped in ice are a much better bet.

One mammoth found in 2013 was still oozing blood, and the meat seemed so fresh that one scientist even took a bite of it. (Note: Do not try this at home.) Biologists have nicknamed the mammoth Buttercup (after some chewed-up flowers they found in her tummy) and have pieced together long fragments of DNA from her cells.

Someday I hope to ride to work every day on my very own woolly mammoth. But even if prehistoric creatures never *literally* come back from the dead, we can still bring them back when we learn about them. We can dig up their bones and study their footprints. Slowly we can paint a picture of what our prehistoric planet was like. That's the miracle of paleontology.

OFFICIAL JUNIOR GENIUS CERTIFICATION EXAM

NAME : _____

DATE : _____

All right, my friends. It's time to put your new paleontological knowledge to the test. Did you know that the graphite in pencils is carbon from long-decayed prehistoric forests? Keep that in mind as you grab your number 2 pencil, and turn the page when I say "Begin."

Wait for it.

Wait for it. . . .

BEGIN.

1. A dinosaur's gizzard served what purpose?

(A) Making sound

(B) Poisoning prey

(C) Detecting smells

(D) Grinding food

2. Which of these plants could have been eaten by the first dinosaurs?

(A) Ferns

(B) Oak trees

(C) Grass

(D) Clover

3. The most unusual thing about *Elasmosaurus* was what overgrown body part?

(A) Its horns

(B) Its wings

(C) Its claws

(D) Its neck

4. The asteroid that killed the dinosaurs made a giant crater off the coast of what part of the world?

(A) Mexico

(B) Australia

(C) Siberia

(D) India

5. *Struthiomimus*, which might have been the fastest dinosaur, looks most like what modern animal?

(A) A rhino

(B) An ostrich

(C) A turtle

(D) A cheetah

6. Where did pioneering British paleontologist Mary Anning hunt for fossils?

(A) In the Gobi Desert   (B) In peat bogs

(C) By the ocean   (D) In rock quarries

7. Plate tectonics is the science that explains the movement of what?

(A) Dinosaur digestion   (B) The continents

(C) Plesiosaurs   (D) Glaciers

8. Each of a *Tyrannosaurus*'s teeth was about the size of what object?

(A) A crayon   (B) A soda can

(C) A banana   (D) A trumpet

9. What would a dinosaur leave behind that might fossilize as coprolites?

(A) Teeth   (B) Dung

(C) Eggs   (D) Footprints

10. Scientists now think most or even all dinosaurs were covered in what?

(A) Spikes   (B) Hair

(C) Feathers   (D) Rich, creamy frosting

11. Which of these were actually true dinosaurs?

(A) Pterosaurs

(B) Hadrosaurs

(C) Ichthyosaurs

(D) Mosasaurs

12. We know from the bony ring in *Velociraptor*'s eye that it could probably do what?

(A) Sleep standing up

(B) See in color

(C) Swim underwater

(D) Hunt at night

13. What name was given to the most famous *Australopithecus* fossil of all time?

(A) Lucy

(B) Lyuba

(C) Bigfoot

(D) Sue

14. The Triassic, Jurassic, and Cretaceous periods make up which geologic era?

(A) Paleozoic

(B) Mesozoic

(C) Cenozoic

(D) Garbanzoic

15. What does the word "dinosaur" mean in Greek?

(A) "Terrible lizard"

(B) "Bird-serpent"

(C) "Ancient reptile"

(D) "Giant reptile"

16. The ankylosaurs were protected from predators by what?

Ⓐ Huge size　　　　　　Ⓑ Powerful tail

Ⓒ Ability to fly　　　　Ⓓ Tanklike armor

17. In 1938, what was discovered about the extinct fish called the coelacanth?

Ⓐ It gave live birth　　Ⓑ It walked on land

Ⓒ It had a spiral jaw　　Ⓓ It was still alive

18. Dinosaurs are divided into ornithischians and saurischians based on the shape of which body part?

Ⓐ Head　　　　　　　Ⓑ Toes

Ⓒ Hips　　　　　　　Ⓓ Tail

19. Compared to today, what was unusual about many mammals of the Pleistocene period?

Ⓐ They laid eggs　　　Ⓑ They lived longer

Ⓒ They were huge　　　Ⓓ They had less fur

20. Which of these is not a long-necked sauropod?

Ⓐ *Allosaurus*　　　　Ⓑ *Diplodocus*

Ⓒ *Brachiosaurus*　　　Ⓓ *Apatosaurus*

All right, pencils down! Turn the page to the answers and see how you did.

ANSWERS

1. ⬭	2. ◿	3. ⬭	4. ◿	5. ⬭
6. ◺	7. ⬭	8. ◺	9. ⬭	10. ◺
11. ⬭	12. ⬭	13. ◿	14. ⬭	15. ◿
16. ⬭	17. ⬭	18. ◺	19. ◺	20. ◿

SCORING

16–20	Certified Junior Genius!
13–15	Nice Try-ceratops
10–12	Can't Win 'Em All-osaurus
6–9	Hot Mess-ozoic
0–5	Extinct

Are you a Certified Junior Genius? You have faced the most terrifying creatures ever to walk the earth—and defeated them. Print out your certificate at JuniorGeniusGuides.com, and someday, you can thank me in your Nobel Prize speech.

If you didn't quite make the cut, don't stress! It doesn't mean you have the golf-ball-size brain of a *Stegosaurus*. You just need a little more time. The dinosaurs lived for more than 100 million years. You can't expect to learn all that in a day! Brush up on your facts and try taking the test again.

HOMEWORK

If you're like most kids I know, you're so excited about dinosaurs that just one day of lessons about them won't be enough. Here are some ideas if you're looking for more pre-hysterical fun.

○ **GO FOSSIL-HUNTING.** You don't have to have a PhD in paleontology to make a fossil discovery. More than 80 percent of fossils are found by accident. *Giganotosaurus* was first discovered by an auto mechanic out for a walk. In 2003, a ten-year-old child found a complete *Torvosaurus* skull in Portugal. Who knows, maybe you'll find something too! (Okay, it probably won't be a dinosaur, but there are lots of other fossils out there.) A local museum, university, or rock club might have ideas on where to look. If you find anything likely-looking, here's a Junior Genius tip: Give it a lick! Fossilized bone is porous, so it will stick slightly to your tongue. Regular rocks won't.

○ **MESOZOIC MEASUREMENTS.** Look up your favorite dinosaur and find out how long it was, head to tail. Find a big field or a long sidewalk and pace off the dinosaur's length. You might mark your imaginary friend by unrolling some twine or tape. How many of you, lying end to end, would it take to equal the same length? If you marked off your dinosaur on blacktop (like at a playground), you can finish up by grabbing a piece of chalk and drawing it on the pavement—life-size!

○ **CRACK THE CODE.** Dinosaur names don't have to be all Greek to you. Here are some dinosaurs whose strange names have cool translations. Spend some time in a library or on the Internet and find out what they mean.

Deinonychus • *Saurophaganax*

Stygimoloch • *Diabloceratops*

Shaochilong • *Teratophoneus*

Enigmosaurus • *Skorpiovenator*

Vulcanodon

○ **DINO-RAMA.** Make your very own prehistoric world by turning a shoe box or cereal box into a diorama. Use real plants and rocks, or color your own. Populate your world with little plastic dinosaur toys, or make your own out of clay or paper. If you're unhappy with your work, you can use a basketball as a meteor and recreate the end-Cretaceous mass extinction.

THE FINAL BELL

Just because class is over doesn't mean you can stop getting smarter, Junior Geniuses! Remember that everyone, from the brainiest know-it-all on down to the tiniest baby, learns things in exactly the same way—one fact at a time, one new discovery at a time. As the great thinker Blaise Pascal said more than four hundred years ago, "It is much better to know something about everything than everything about something."

In fact, if you keep your eyes and ears open, you can probably learn something new every hour of every day—for your entire life. Maybe someday you'll be such a famous genius that the next generation of Junior Geniuses will salute *your* picture instead of Albert Einstein's!

If so, please consider keeping your hair more neatly combed than Professor Einstein did.

Class dismissed!

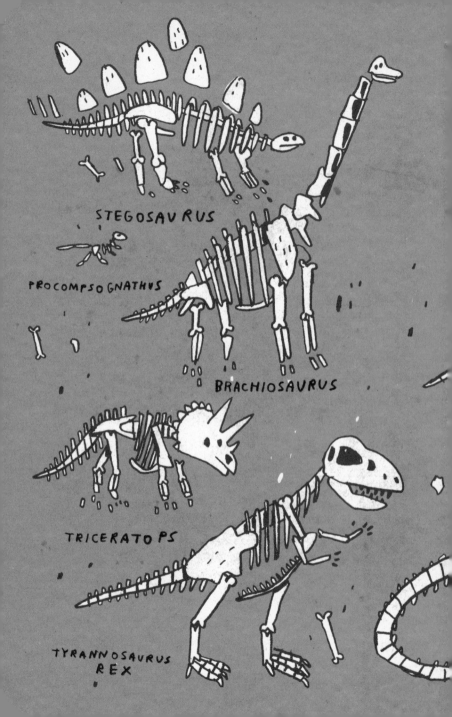

STEGOSAURUS

PROCOMPSOGNATHUS

BRACHIOSAURUS

TRICERATOPS

TYRANNOSAURUS
REX